There are many ways to commemorate the American Revolution. Perhaps none is more significant than pondering the issues of the moment and deciding to implement in our time the policies so eloquently heralded in the Declaration of Independence—equality, life, liberty, and the pursuit of happiness.

As Christians, we believe and witness to the conviction that:

- People are more important than programs.
- Justice is to be valued before security.
- Equality for all people is to be cherished before any private fortune.
- Liberation is more important than the establishment of political power.
- Peace is to be sought before national prestige.
- The church cannot be prescribed or limited by any political boundaries.

America has been willing to modify her way of life as long as it hasn't affected her pursuit of wealth or national power. If America is going to survive, a change of her ways is imperative.

A DREAM FOR AMERICA

John A. Lapp

Introduction by Senator Mark O. Hatfield

CHOICE
BOOKS

Published by Herald Press, a division of Mennonite
Publishing House, for Mennonite Broadcasts, Inc.

A DREAM FOR AMERICA

A CHOICE BOOK
Published by Herald Press, a division of Mennonite Publishing House, for Mennonite Broadcasts, Inc. Manufactured by Pillar Books.

Copyright © 1976 by Herald Press, Scottdale, Pa. 15683

Library of Congress Catalog Card Number: 75-44612

International Standard Book Number: 0-8361-1796-4

Choice Books edition, June 1976

Choice Books are distributed by Mennonite Broadcasts, Inc., Harrisonburg, Virginia 22801. The word "Choice" and corresponding symbol are registered in the United States Patent Office.

To the men and women of the Mennonite Central Committee who have been demonstrating a better way.

CONTENTS

A DREAM FOR AMERICA

INTRODUCTION

We tend to put the United States of America beyond the reach of God's judgment. The words on the back of our Great Seal read, "God hath ordained our undertakings." Our money is emblazoned with "In God We Trust." Our leaders solemnly invoke the name of God in their political speeches. We earnestly want to believe that ours is God's chosen land, that we are His chosen people, and that the leaders we have are divinely chosen and given special wisdom.

This impulse is born out of our own lives. We would rather believe that we merit God's blessing than admit that we stand under His judgment, and in need of His forgiveness. But however difficult it is to admit our sin, the evidence of it is all around us, in the personal dilemmas of our lives and in the crises that afflict our nation. The Apostle John reminds us that—

> If we refuse to admit that we are sinners, then we live in a world of illusion and truth becomes a stranger to us. 1 John 1:10

Continued belief in national self-righteousness,

therefore, no matter what we as a nation do, only leads us into greater peril.

Many believe that our security comes through our materialism, our wealth, and our gross national product. So we despoil our environment and neglect the quality of man's spirit in order to expand our materialistic self-indulgence.

We are now capable of destroying most of the world's population in a few moments through the power of nuclear warfare. We operate on the assumption that human life is expendable, and rationalize this axiom on the sole basis that this is what our enemy believes, so this must be our belief also.

On the eve of our nation's Bicentennial year evangelist Billy Graham challenged the American public to engage in "humiliation, fasting, and prayer," as a beginning of the celebration of the birth of the nation.

Graham echoes the words of others in our nation's past who recognized that blessing from God was not as a result of religious tradition or prideful accomplishment, but dependence upon God for guidance in the paths of righteousness.

The Puritan John Winthrop said in 1630,

For we must consider that we shall be a city upon a hill. The eyes of all people are upon us, so that if we shall deal falsely without God in this work we have undertaken, and so cause Him to withdraw His present help from us, we shall be made a story and a byword through the world.

President Abraham Lincoln had a profound sense of

the sovereignty of God. He knew how the nation stood accountable to God's judgment. In the midst of the Civil War, the U.S. Senate requested, and Lincoln responded on three separate occasions to a resolution setting aside a day for national humiliation, fasting, and prayer.

Seeing the effects of a nation torn apart, President Lincoln did not appeal to any pretentious image of national self-righteousness; rather, he called the nation to repentance. He believed that only through the acknowledgment of our corporate guilt and confession of national sins could the country regain its national purpose and unity. Lincoln recognized that though the nation had prospered, "We have forgotten God." Because the nation had begun to believe that it had flourished through its own superior wisdom and virtue, Lincoln stated,

It behooves us . . . to humble ourselves before the offended Power, to confess our national sins, and to pray for clemency and forgiveness.

In the midst of the Bicentennial, John Lapp provides us, in this book, with another reminder that our celebration is to be one of responsible action not merely frivolous jubilance.

If we trace our religious heritage, as the Church of Jesus Christ rightly will do, we err in simply branding our nation as "Christian." We must look afresh at the definition of the word "Christian." What determines whether or not a nation or any group is acting in a "Christian" manner? Can the word "Christian" even be applied to a nation? And does not the gospel of Jesus Christ include God's judgment and justice in addition to mercy and blessing? Because some of our leaders have acknowledged God's sovereignty does not mean that we have, as a nation, conducted ourselves in a manner befitting the term "Christian."

Unfortunately, it is more comfortable to believe in the spiritual symbols of righteousness than to acknowledge the reality and presence of evil in ourselves and in our corporate life. So we become adroit at manipulating religious impulses in our land to sanctify our national life.

We are in need of repentance. Our claims of righteousness, as individuals, and as a nation, deceive only ourselves. We should remember the words of the prophet Amos:

I hate, I despise your feasts, and your solemn assemblies, I will not accept them: neither will I regard the peace offerings of your fat beasts. Take away from me the noise of your songs, for I will not hear the melody of your viols. But let justice roll down like water, and righteousness like an ever-flowing stream. Amos 5:21-24.

Why this emphasis upon the need for humiliation and repentance? A celebration of our history can be productive and positive if we begin from the proper starting point. The church can, indeed, lead our country to experience God's blessings, but we must open our eyes to the realities of our national life and conduct.

A Dream for America helps us see beyond our traditional understanding of the application of the gospel to the condition of man. The righteousness that exalts a nation applies not only to our individual piety but to our national policies in the areas of race, international justice, and equal justice under law.

It is my firm conviction that a genuine spirit of repentance, infecting the climate of our nation at all levels, can heal the wounds that presently afflict us. Reconciliation of the divisions and animosities that exist among our people can occur once there is a mutual acknowledgment of this need for contrition, which allows human compassion to grow.

There is hope for a land and a people who have the capacity to recognize their sins and their faults, and turn from them. Repentance means precisely this—to turn the other way. In so doing, we recognize that past events and present conditions cannot be rationalized or justified; rather, they must be repented of, so a whole new way can be sought. This is how individuals and how our land as a whole can seek authentic renewal and transformation.

Mark O. Hatfield
United States Senator

January 6, 1976
Washington, D.C.

AUTHOR'S PREFACE

*Of Issachar men who had understanding of
the times, to know what Israel ought to do.
1 Chronicles 12:32.*

This pithy biblical description provides a launching
pad for these essays. "Understanding the times" has
been a passion of people from the days of the ancient
astrologer to the modern newspaper commentator.
Enormous amounts of money and energy are put into
market research and public policy analysis by individuals and organizations who need to know, like ancient
Israel, what they "ought to do."

To profess to understand the times is both presump-
tuous and dangerous. As long as people, governments,
corporations, and private institutions have some
freedom of choice, no one can say with exactitude what
is indeed going on. Yet we humans have the need to
know so we can plan our travel, decide our careers,
program our business, and develop public policies. But
it must be emphasized from the beginning that this
knowledge will be inexact. "Understanding the times"
also means a recognition of limits. Peter Berger re-

17

cently observed that "all political action takes place in a context of inadequate information and inability to foresee the future." Understanding must then include "the postulate of ignorance"—recognizing the unforeseen, the contingent, the ironical.

The bicentennial of the United States is an occasion for probing not only the meaning of the American past, but also the global present. If one of the givens of the American experience is broad participation in decision making and widespread debate regarding public policies, then each citizen needs some understanding of the times. We might paraphrase the scripture to say, "Americans need to understand the times to know what the United States ought to do." Paulo Friere, the Brazilian Christian educator, observes that people are mere objects, onlookers, adapters to history, unless they "grasp the themes." Only then can they hope to intervene in reality.

The author believes the most important ingredient of a commemoration of this nation's birthday would be a serious search to "understand the times" during this bicentennial epoch. More important than reenactments of the past, though interesting in themselves, is the hard study of issues that late twentieth-century people must confront if there are to be future centennial celebrations. More important than pilgrimages, though a profitable source of historical understanding, is debate over issues critical to community and national survival. More important than celebration, though essential to community solidarity, is decision and action to guarantee the continuation and expansion of the open society we all cherish.

These essays are intended to stimulate and suggest. They cannot be comprehensive or definitive. Here are interpretations and some factual details. The author's point of view will be obvious: Christian, pacifistic, global, hopeful, realistic. Readers are encouraged to determine their own point of view and decide on their own course of action. Chapters 1, 5, 9, and 10 are broadly interpretative. The other chapters focus on single topics or issues.

I am grateful to Mennonite Broadcasts, Inc., especially Ronald Yoder, former director of Choice Books, for encouraging me to write this volume. Readers of the column on current affairs in *Christian Living* for the past thirteen years will observe many ideas first expressed on those pages. Paul M. Schrock, book editor of Herald Press, has been both encouraging and helpful in refining the readability of the volume. Professors J. Daniel Hess and Theron Schlabach, of the Goslien College enriched the essays by their critical comments. Alice W. Lapp not only typed the entire manuscript more than once but added her own concerns in clarity and understandability.

Ideas or even language are never the author's alone. It is impossible to name all the sources of information or each of those persons who have contributed to my own understanding. I hope those who find a quotation from their writing or a germ of their thought in these pages will consider it an extension of their influence. My apologies to those not properly recognized. In the interest of readability no footnotes have been used, but the sources are all included in the reading list at the back of the book.

Three enjoyable years of my life were spent on the staff of the Peace Section of Mennonite Central Committee, Akron, Pennsylvania. MCC, as it is popularly known, calls itself "a Christian resource for meeting human need." It is in that spirit I want these essays to be read—a modest recognition of the bicentennial, as MCC always says, "In the Name of Christ."

John A. Lapp

1.

The future of America depends on...

DECIDING OUR FUTURE TOGETHER

It seems to have been reserved to the people of this country ... to decide ... whether societies ... are really capable or not of establishing good government from reflection and choice or whether they are forever destined to depend on their political constitutions or accident and force.—Alexander Hamilton.

We suggested in the Preface that the bicentennial epoch should be an occasion for new study and fresh understandings of the contemporary human situation. One of the first essentials for understanding is a sense of history: a recognition that the experience of the past is important, but that profound differences distinguish the world of 1776 from the world of 1976.

In 1776, 3½ million people lived in the thirteen colonies. Today we are 220 million strong. Then we were an eastern seaboard people. Now we are a continental people. In 1776 these thirteen colonies were quite isolated from the rest of the world. They were bounded by the ocean and the mountains. Today this country has a global influence and it affects and is affected by every nation on earth.

In 1776 this country was largely made up of three groups of people The English were the dominant majority. Blacks, mostly slaves, accounted for more than a fifth of the population. Germans, Dutch, and French were sizeable minorities. Today the Anglo majority includes almost all the Europeans, who have been assimilated, except those who speak Spanish. The British/German/Black spectrum of 1776 has evolved into the English/Spanish/Black grouping of today.

In 1776 this country was highly decentralized. The most important place for all people was their local community. A man was from a county before he was from a state, and certainly before he was from the United States. In 1976 one's identity largely comes from the nation. Washington is now more important than Philadelphia or Boston for most people. A generally rural society has become a highly industrialized one.

In 1776 the general spirit was largely peaceful. Where there was conflict and hostility, as on the frontier and even during the Revolution, only a small percentage of the population was involved. In 1976 sizeable parts of our economy, ideology, and work force are dominated by military considerations. Some people are inclined to compare the statesmen of the Revolutionary epoch—Washington, Adams, Franklin, and Jefferson—to the absence of giants in our time.

Perhaps the most significant point about 1776 is the optimism and the hope of that generation. John Adams, second President of the United States and one of the more profound thinkers of the eighteenth century, said, "I always consider the settlement of America as the opening of a grand scheme and design in Providence for the illumination of the ignorant and the emancipation of the slavish part of mankind all over the earth."

Seventeen seventy-six was perceived not as something that took place in the colonies alone. It was seen as the beginning of an age of revolution which included Western Europe. Certainly 1789 in France is directly related to 1776 in the United States. Political and social changes in Britain, though they came a little later, were intimately related to the American Revolution. All during the nineteenth century and well into the twentieth century, the longing of peoples throughout the world for freedom and home rule, the revolutionary hope, has been nurtured by the example of the American colonies.

We cannot overemphasize the extent to which America became the hope for the whole world. The early Americans were a highly subversive lot. When Jefferson and Franklin went to Europe, they immediately became the heroes of the people who wanted to change those societies. Until very recently revolutionary movements in nearly every country looked for inspiration to the American prototype. In the late 1940s, when Vietnam tried to declare its independence from the French, they took as their model the Declaration of Independence. Their heroes were the heroes of the American Revolutionary epoch.

We ought also to recognize the idealism of the eighteenth century. The intellectual leaders were very optimistic and highly idealistic. One needs only to go back and read the Declaration again to recognize the elegance of their claims—all men created equal, all people have rights to life, liberty, and the pursuit of happiness. The purpose of government is to secure these rights. When the government no longer performs this function, it is incumbent upon the people to change the government.

A second characteristic of 1776 was the profound belief in a higher law. The 1776 revolutionaries believed in a government of laws based on the moral law of the universe. E. S. Corwin in his book *The Higher Law Background of the American Constitutional Law* describes the theological and philosophical appeals to providence and to the laws of nature and nature's God. The constitutional dimensions of this Revolution are important in suggesting the rule of law and the concept of limited government.

A third observation is that the Revolution was a social movement. John Adams said, "The issue was not only who should rule but who should rule at home." It was revolutionary to disestablish churches, to abolish hereditary titles, to curb the military establishment, to overthrow colonial governments, to establish popular education, and to popularize the notion of a classless and a casteless society.

These are some of the less recognized revolutionary achievements worthy of commemoration. Add to this the influential struggle for religious freedom in most of the colonies. The American Revolution was not only a political affair but also a social and religious process. It restructured the economy, ending many taxes and other kinds of payments to English officials and landholders.

Finally, it is worth noting that the American Revolution was never completed. The noble insights and claims that were made in the Declaration, the writings of the Federalists, and the Constitution were not easily achieved. Some of the thoughtful men of that generation were aware, for instance, that slavery could not be justified in a free society. Many were conscious of the shabby treatment of the Indians and of the poor. An agenda remained for future generations.

Nevertheless, the American Revolution was an important event in the history of the world. Alexis de Tocqueville said, when he visited the United States fifty years later, "I have seen the future and it works." He became one of the justifiers and promoters of the Revolution beyond this country. The American forefathers were the first people, according to Abraham Lincoln, "to bring forth a new nation," to create a new

25

society out of a variety of nationality groups. So 1776 is not only a significant event for Americans, but a milestone in world history.

Interestingly, the most important motif in the United States in the late 1970s appears to be counterrevolution rather than revolution. The nature of every revolution is to set up a counterrevolution. According to students of the American Revolution, a counterrevolution already occurred at the Constitutional Convention of 1787. There certainly were anti-revolutionary fears in the thoughts of John Randolph and Alexander Hamilton.

Others, like Thomas Jefferson, were revolutionaries through and through. He considered bankers more dangerous than armies, newspapers more important than governments. James Madison, his protégé, said, "The truth is that all men having power should be distrusted." Jefferson and Madison in some respects appear to have felt like Stalin and Mao who desired a perpetual revolution. This didn't happen for many good reasons, but the question for the 1970s is whether Americans have flipped to the other side and now tend to support those forces which prevent freedom and equality from developing.

The movement toward counterrevolution is partially a natural development. When a society or individual gains power, influence, and wealth, it is natural to protect and preserve it. The nature of power is self-preservation. Now that America enjoys tremendous power, wealth, and investments, our main urge is to protect and preserve. President Kennedy once said, "America is now the watchman on the walls of world freedom."

That philosophy can easily be interpreted to justify American military intervention to preserve American interests in the Cubas and Vietnams of the world. Lyndon Johnson said it more crassly: "There are 3 billion people in the world and we have only 200 million of them. We are outnumbered 15 to 1. If might did make right they would sweep over the United States and take what we have. We have what they want." The United States Army, the Marines, the CIA, and diplomats at the United Nations support counterrevolutionary activity in an effort to protect what we have which poorer people want. This is why many persons now see the United States as a counterrevolutionary nation.

Forces and movements within the United States symbolize both revolution and counterrevolution. The Civil Rights Movement of the 1950s and 1960s clearly chose to expand the implications of the ideals set forth in 1776. The plea for a redress of grievances was a request to live up to the American ideal itself. On the other hand, some groups in the United States trying to defend the American system are ready to sacrifice the Constitution itself to preserve their own status and power. Right-wing political groups shout, "America, right or wrong," in an attempt to squelch critical voices of any kind.

The essence of a free society is the ability to make choices and the courage to choose. The bicentennial era is a time to remember and reflect on those decisions we collectively call the American Revolution. Between 1770 and 1790 the thirteen colonies decided to break the tie with the British government and declare national independence. During this time each colony and the nation itself designed new constitutions and new structures of government. During these years decisions were made for national expansion across the Appalachians. In addition to fundamental political choices, new social structures involving patterns of land ownership, separation of church and state, and public education emerged. The decision to abolish slavery was reached in several states, but not in all of them.

History, from one point of view, is the story of the human family individually and collectively making choices. The notion of a free society presumes the ability and the desire to choose. The concept of democratic government implies that decisions are continually being made about those big issues which determine the direction of human affairs as well as about the smaller issues which determine the quality of life of the participants.

From 1776 to 1976 the American people have chosen 94 Congresses and 38 Presidents. The people have sometimes called for strong leadership and decisive action. At other times they have been content to let others determine their destiny. In addition to the choice of leadership, masses of people have on some occasions demanded war and at other times have called for peace. Some have urged the abolition of slavery and others have fought to preserve slavery. In recent times the people have discussed and sometimes chosen between civil liberties and repression, discrimination and civil rights, reform and violent change, militarism and internationalism, ignoring the poor and abolishing poverty, war and peace in Indochina.

These choices have sometimes been obvious. At other times they have occurred through inaction rather than by deliberate and studied proposals. Whatever its character or shape, the act of choosing lies at the heart of the American style of life and government. But the difficulties of making such choices become greater all the time. Sheer numbers alone mean that not all people become part of the choosing process. Educational institutions, churches, corporations, the media, and governmental units themselves participate in the process, making individual action more and more difficult. The complexity and size of issues oftimes dwarf the individual capacity to understand and decide.

Yet decide we must if freedom and democracy are to have meaning. Bicentennial reflections could not come at a more appropriate time, for the 1970s and 1980s are generating issues in many respects as weighty as those of the Revolution itself. The issues today include:

Style of government: Can there be freedom and democracy when the issues are global and not merely national?

Quality of life: Can there be life, liberty, and the pursuit of happiness when millions live at the edge of existence and the border between the rich and poor becomes a gaping canyon?

The possibility of the future itself: Can people survive the threat of nuclear holocaust and environmental disintegration?

The bicentennial follows more than a decade of traumatic upheaval. Since the assassination of John F. Kennedy on November 22, 1963, there have been half a dozen other attacks on prominent officials. Since then massive mobilizations of opposition have challenged public policies on race relations, poverty, and the war in Indochina. Students have occupied university buildings, broken the power of administrators, and seen their comrades killed by the national guard. Dozens of cities have erupted in violent destruction as houses, jobs, service, and human rights seemed dwarfed by the reality of oppression. One President was forced to give up seeking another term, and another left under the cloud of impeachment as cabinet members and staff were indicted for disobeying laws and circumventing the Constitution.

In this context the bicentennial becomes an occasion to ask again with Alexander Hamilton whether the people of the United States can establish "good government from reflection and choice or whether they are forever destined to depend . . . on accident and force." There are many ways to commemorate the American Revolution but perhaps none is more significant than pondering the issues of the moment and deciding to implement in our time the policies so eloquently heralded in the Declaration of Independence—equality, life, liberty, and the pursuit of happiness.

2.

The future of America depends on...

WORKING TOWARD EQUALITY AND
JUSTICE FOR ALL

*Certain fundamental matters are clear....
The racial attitude and behavior of white
Americans toward black Americans ... has
shaped our history decisively; it now
threatens to affect our future.—Report of the
National Advisory Commission on Civil
Disorders, 1968.*

There is no time like the bicentennial to reconsider the
problem of inequality that has persisted from the be-
ginnings of the American republic. Even before the
Revolution, the American Indian was being driven
from colony to wilderness and beyond. Even before the
American Revolution, black Americans were reduced
from indentured servants with hopes of freedom to
chattel slavery. Since the Revolution, inequality has
persisted.

The experiences of blacks, reds, and browns (the
Spanish American of recent awareness) is a persistent
reminder that the ideals of the revolutionaries remain
more rhetoric than reality 200 years later. Eighty percent of the 800,000 American Indians live in poverty.

Seventy-five percent of the 22 million black Americans live in urban slums. The vast majority of the 7.5 million Mexican Americans are poor, undereducated, and discriminated against because of their color and language.

All of these groups have mobilized their forces to redress their grievances. They have used the arguments of the Declaration of Independence and the Constitution to claim rights and freedoms the majority of Americans have long claimed and eulogized. Each of these movements began in protest but moved to politics based on black power, brown power, and red power.

The central issue in the most recent conflict over the role of minorities in American life is the same concern that began the past two decades of civil rights controversy—schools. This time the question is the use of buses to transport children to equalize educational opportunities. Busing has generated local controversy in such places as Charlotte, Richmond, Pontiac, Boston, and Louisville. Federal courts have shown that schools in these cities have deliberately been located in the center rather than at the boundaries of segregated residential areas for the express purpose of preserving school segregation.

The same courts have ordered school busing to overcome the inadequacies of segregated education. Chief Justice Burger in the celebrated case of *Swann* vs. *Charlotte-Mecklinberg*, April 1971, held that "school authorities should make every effort to achieve the greatest possible degree of actual desegregation." This may require bus transportation as "desegregation plans cannot be limited to the walk-in school."

The question of busing hits the raw nerve of a society that has institutionalized separate racial patterns not only in schools but in housing and employment. The solution to the problems of racial separation will not be found in perpetuating such separation but in destroying the old patterns and developing new ones. The school bus, unfortunately, is caught in the cross fire.

Forty percent of American children ride to school in a bus. An additional twenty-five percent depend on public transportation. During the 1970–71 school year, 20 million elementary and secondary school children were bused. They rode 256,000 yellow buses 2.2 billion miles at a cost of $1.5 billion. Almost the only children who do not ride a bus are those within walking distance of their school.

Senator Mondale (D-Minn.) says the issue isn't "to bus or not to bus, but whether we will build on successful examples to make school desegregation work."

Children have been bused since the 1920s when educators decided education would be enhanced in larger, consolidated units. That process has continued to the point where a reaction now appears to be setting in. Some school districts are now opting for smaller units. Even so, many suburban communities are building large educational parks for a variety of educational experiences. Some of these are consciously being built to overcome existing segregated patterns.

While schools were consolidating from 1920–54, many new schools took shape along segregated patterns. Often black students were bused from one county to another, passing three or four white schools to preserve racial purity.

No one has ordered indiscriminate busing. In only a few places has busing been ordered across district lines. The courts have been slow to require busing, although they have recognized that segregated education means inferior schooling. Some twenty-one years ago in the famous case of *Brown* vs. *Board of Education*, the Supreme Court first ruled that "separate and unequal" schools are unconstitutional. Since that historic decision, study after study has shown that integrated education can mean better education for all children, white as well as black, rich as well as poor.

Busing is not the real issue, because most students are already bused. Few students should expect to be bused for purposes of integration alone. If such busing is necessary, it is because school boards and zoning boards have deliberately created segregated institutions which require busing to overcome local barriers to equal education.

Ten lawyers from the civil rights divison of the Department of Justice observed this sham before in the spring of 1972. They concluded that "the recent fervor in the area of busing is nothing more than a thinly veiled attempt to sacrifice the rights of minority children to racist pressure groups and political expedience. . . . What we have been witnessing," they said, "is an attempted rollback, a camouflaged effort to resurrect the concept of 'separate but equal.' "

Politicians, of course, can find issues where issues don't exist. They will cultivate fears to generate votes. This is precisely what is happening. Columnist Nicholas von Hoffman put it crudely: "If Congress can't keep blacks in the back of the bus, then don't let 'em ride at all."

The busing controversy has been fueled first and foremost by those who have refused to accept the constitutional and moral developments of the past twenty years. Here is a new place to stand to defend the immoral and unconstitutional status quo. Governor Wallace said fifteen years ago that no blacks would darken the door of the University of Alabama. He lost that battle. In busing he has simply found a new line of defense.

This time the segregationists have discovered new allies in the Northern cities and suburbs whose hypocrisy has finally been unmasked. The hatreds in Boston have been every bit as volatile and bitter as those in Birmingham.

What has been lacking as the busing controversy has grown is any kind of moral leadership. The congressional leadership and the executive branch have fallen over themselves to devise legislative and administrative ways to capture what they believe is the anti-busing vote. A constitutional amendment to prevent busing has been proposed. Former President Nixon went to the airwaves to propose an "Equal Educational Opportunities Act" in order "to end segregation in a way that does not result in more busing." The President proposed an immediate moratorium on busing and specifically stated that courts would be forbidden to require busing of students in the sixth grade or below if the average distance to be traveled in the aggregate exceeded that traveled the year before. No other

President has dared such an assault on the Constitution and courts since the post-Civil War epoch.

The debate over busing more than any recent issue suggests the depth of racist thinking and practice in the United States. It also unveils the shallow commitment of many (if not most) Americans to the vision of racial equality. Whether the controversy or new legislation will have any great effect will depend on whether the national commitment to racial equality can continue and be expanded.

In 1968 the National Advisory Commission on Civil Disorders suggested that "white racism" has been the major force in creating the instability of American society. More recently Theodore Hesburgh, president of Notre Dame University and a member of the U.S. Commission on Civil Rights, observed that "white racism is the attitude that cries, 'We approve your goals, but we deplore your process; we approve your ends, but deplore your means.'"

The busing controversy highlights the contemporary form of the struggle for equality. Thirty years ago the eminent Swedish economist Gunnar Myrdal produced the most comprehensive survey of race relations ever written. Myrdal in *An American Dilemma* observed America at a crossroads with two alternatives. One was to practice what she preached. All people would be treated as truly equal with equal opportunities to life, liberty, and the pursuit of happiness. This would result in the interracial society proposed in the 18th century by the Quaker John Woolman, by the abolitionists and the Radical Republicans in the 1860's, and the democratic society supposedly fought for during the world wars of the twentieth century.

The other alternative was to continue being the society she actually was, a country of two societies—one rich, one poor; one black, one white; one believing in its superiority, the other relegated to inferior status. This alternative, Myrdal believed, would finally mean a system with extensive barricades to prevent the advancement of the Negro American.

We no longer have just an American dilemma. We have an American tragedy. A tragedy is a drama, an artistic creation, that describes a series of events in the life of a person or a group which ends in an unhappy catastrophe. Some nations, like people, are born to greatness as was Hamlet or they have visions of greatness as did Prometheus. Yet they end in miserable despair and humiliation. The beginning of wisdom for all Americans is to realize the depth of their tragic existence. The essence of tragedy is catastrophe bred in the excess of success.

America has a rich democratic tradition, perhaps more freedom and opportunity than any other country. But it has been blinded by color and culture. Those who are not like the majority have been too often relegated to perpetual inferiority. Racism is used to defend status and wealth. Property becomes more important than life.

The tragedy of America is that she has been hypocritical. She has prophesied for public consumption a style of life she really didn't intend for anyone. She has been willing to modify her way of life as long as it hasn't affected her pursuit of wealth or national power.

She piously passes civil rights laws but refuses to support their enforcement or devote the energy necessary to create an equal democracy for all her citizens.

If America is going to survive, she must honestly face the tragic elements of her existence. A change of her ways is imperative. The beginning of this change can only come in self-understanding. Jesus lamented, in a similar situation, "O Jerusalem, Jerusalem. . . . Behold, your house is forsaken and desolate." Later he told the Jerusalem women, "Weep not for me, but for yourselves and your children."

3.

The Future of America depends on. . .

SHARING THE WORLD'S RESOURCES

Whatever our ideological belief or social structure, we are part of a single international economic system on which all of our national economic objectives depend. No nation or bloc of nations can unilaterally determine the shape of the future.—Henry A. Kissinger.

Perhaps there is no more striking difference between 1776 and 1976 than the global involvements of the United States. The daily news includes data from all the continents. American corporations and traders operate in nearly all 128 member-countries of the United Nations. The typical household depends on energy from the Middle East, foods from Latin America, and metals from Africa. The catchword of the American Revolution—independence—no longer seems quite suitable during the bicentennial. Perhaps the most important consideration today is whether Americans can see themselves as part of a larger world to whom they have responsibilities or whether they continue to extol the virtues of independence and autonomy.

Though the recent energy crisis has made us aware of interdependence, most persons do not recognize how dependent human welfare is on the raw materials, productivity, and well-being of other nations. Throughout human history nations have engaged in trade with each other. But the increasingly unified global economy of our time also includes international financial flow, an international monetary system, energy interdependence, a global technology market, tourism, and multinational industrial production.

So essential are the products, raw materials, tourists, and technology of many nations to other nations that the old idea of national sovereignty is being traded off for economic prosperity. No country or even continent has all the raw materials needed for a modern industrial plant. By 1985 the United States will depend on imports for more than half of nine basic industrial raw materials. These include aluminum, chromium, lead, nickel, manganese, tin, zinc, and iron.

The energy shortage tells us something about other kinds of shortages and crises that are bound to emerge in the years ahead. Oil and energy are especially graphic examples of interdependence. Thirty-five percent of the world's energy fields cross national borders. With petroleum consumption climbing at the rate of 3 to 4 percent per year, the United States depends more on imports for a high percentage of its needs. A few Middle Eastern countries now control over half the world's known oil reserves.

Another major evidence of interdependence is the multinational corporation. Such an organization's production, sales, capital, technology, and management come from and serve more than one country. United States-based multinational corporations produce 4 times more goods abroad than are exported, some $70 billion worth per year. Approximately one-tenth of the U. S. gross national product comes from investment abroad.

Indeed, nearly one fifth of the entire world's economic product is generated by international companies. In comparing the gross national products and the gross annual sales of multinational companies, 59 of the 100 largest economic units are multinational companies. General Motors' annual sales of over $25 billion are larger than the gross national products of Switzerland and South Africa. Many of the large corporations' sales are growing more rapidly than entire national economies.

Global interdependence is not merely economic. Worldwide communications and transportation systems provide the framework for new political structures that may inevitably emerge to satisfy the needs of the new situation.

In the past, the relationship of oil and food reserves was not often considered. But the stark facts are that while Western Europe, Japan, and North America face shortages of oil, large portions of Africa, Latin America, and Asia are on the verge of mass starvation due to the shortages of food. Addeke Boerma, director general of the United Nations Food and Agriculture Organization, says the Sahel nations—the semidesert region just south of the Sahara—need twice as much food grains as are presently available (300,000 tons) to halt widespread starvation and malnutrition. Dr. Norman Borlaug, the Nobel Prize winner for his work in developing seeds essential to the Green Revolution, suggests that upward of 20 million persons around the world will needlessly die during this decade because of the reduction in fertilizer production due to fuel shortages.

Lester Brown, author of *World Without Borders,* points out that "the United States and Canada today control a larger share of the world's exportable supplies of grains than the Middle East does of oil." This being the case, Mr. Kissinger is precisely correct in noting that oil and food do go together. "How can we," the secretary of state asks, "expect cooperation on oil if we will not cooperate to relieve hunger?" We might even suggest the world food situation relates in some way to North America's dependence on copper, tin, magnesium, and the numerous other resources.

Before adopting a posture of interdependence, Americans will have to modify our tradition of independence and revolutionize our public policies. It will not be easy to educate our national reflexes and instincts. Ironically, former President Nixon's response to the energy crises was called Project Independence.

President Ford, in an early 1975 NBC television interview, commented on the threat of another oil embargo. "We are not going to permit America to be strangled to death," he declared emphatically. "Military action against oil-producing nations may be necessary for our self-preservation. . . . Wars have been fought over natural resources from time immemorial."

At the same time as the image of strangulation has entered the public vocabulary, another word, "triage," has come to symbolize the public response to world famine.

In 1975, while the executive branch hinted and threatened military action on oil, a United States House of Representatives agriculture subcommittee asked, "Will you and I as American citizens someday have to participate in the choice of 'Food Triage'?"

Triage is a battlefield term sometimes used to separate the wounded into three categories: (1) those who will survive without medical help; (2) those who will probably survive with medical help; and (3) those likely not to survive even with treatment. Some persons who sense the desperation of the world food shortage suggest the world must be divided in a similar way. Certain countries and provinces simply can't survive, so food aid should be directed to those who probably can.

This kind of cold, calculated thinking is not new. Sword-rattling militarists who threaten and cajole in their lust for power and influence are always with us. Others speak with detachment of famine as a natural force which will eliminate the millions who are unfortunate enough to be born where there is insufficient food, medicine, and shelter. Together notions of war for oil and triage for food suggest the enormous dimensions of the power struggle that lies ahead.

One reason why the continual war of nerves and escalation of armaments in the Middle East is so portentous is the danger of precisely this kind of thinking. If a fifth Arab-Israeli war erupts, it may be hard for the United States not to expand the conflict to Libya or Kuwait. This will be especially so if the image of strangulation moves from the realm of rhetoric and becomes a believable public myth.

In 1967, William and Paul Paddock wrote a book entitled *Famine–1975*. Many persons thought these brothers unduly pessimistic. This reality, however, is upon us. A.H. Boerma, director-general of the United Nations Food and Agriculture Organizations, expected 10 million persons to die of starvation in 1975 and 400–600 million more to suffer from severe malnourishment.

The Paddocks proposed selecting certain countries for assistance and ignoring others based on the triage idea. The countries not to be assisted are "nations in which the population growth trend has already passed the agricultural potential. This, combined with inadequate leadership and other divisive factors, makes catastrophic disasters inevitable. . . . To send food to them is to throw sand in the ocean."

The enormity of the food problem certainly lends itself to this attitude. Since 1967 we've seen that the highly publicized Green Revolution is no permanent miracle and that enormous food reserves can quickly disappear.

Simultaneous with repeated suggestions for intervention in the oil-producing countries have been the conferences, reports, and articles grappling with the realities of hunger. In a *Newsweek* essay, California lawyer Johnson C. Montgomery declared that "famine is one of nature's ways of telling profligate people that they have been irresponsible in their breeding habits." With the future of mankind at stake, he suggested "the United States should remain an island of plenty in a sea of hunger" in order to "protect the material and intellectual seed grain for the future. The future is "my children. . . . Don't ask me to cut my children back on anything. I won't do it without a fight."

The most vigorous spokesman for this point of view is biologist Garrett Hardin who in various articles has made a case against helping the poor. Hardin uses the metaphor of the lifeboat to describe the developed countries. Thousands of people swim in the surrounding sea, trying to climb aboard. The lifeboat has a limited capacity. The issue, then, is who is allowed into the boat, the only means of survival, and who decides who is allowed in.

After considering the many factors that go into making life worth living—food, air, water, forests, beaches, wildlife, scenery, and solitude—Hardin comments that the harsh ethics of the lifeboat will become even harsher if the food problem is resolved without corresponding change in population growth rates and an enforced world environmental policy. "Without a true world government to control reproduction and the use of available resources the sharing ethic . . . is impossible. In the foreseeable future our survival demands that we govern our actions by the ethics of the lifeboat. . . ."

Like the threat of war over oil, triage is far too simple a concept. There are not starving nations but starving people. No nation as a whole but parts of nations are famine areas. Triage also assumes there is an elite which can determine the fate of peoples and nations, indeed of the world. Which elite does the job? It also assumes that nothing can be done about hunger.

But famine is not a necessity. Indeed if presently known techniques were used worldwide, there would be no famine.

Images of strangulation and triage suggest there are no alternatives to an admittedly unjust situation. Self-interest mandates war, threats of war, hunger, and famine. Hardin puts it most crassly: "The boat swamps, everyone drowns. Complete justice, complete catastrophe."

Yet there are other ways. First of all, we must ask if this analysis is correct. Must the United States have Arab oil? Actually we import more oil from Nigeria and Venezuela than from all the Arab states combined. No one suggests invading these countries! Questions can also be raised about the realism of trusting the judgment of military thinkers who failed so abysmally in Vietnam.

We must ask Garrett Hardin and the Paddocks if they are using valid metaphors. Are the United States and Canada lifeboats or luxury liners? The grain used in the manufacture of alcoholic beverages alone could eliminate the food shortage in whole countries now verging on starvation. The question then is not one of production but of usage and distribution.

More disturbing than the factual issues raised in this chapter is the character and quality of this kind of thinking. Such self-centered and self-justifying thinking has brought the world to the brink of disaster. The issue is the world view of many opinion makers, including supposed statesmen and scholars.

The quadrupling of oil prices in 1974, we are told, marked a turning point in history, one of the two or three signal developments of the post World War II era. If so, this also requires a new kind of thinking and a new view of global interdependence.

Strangulation, triage, and the lifeboat ethic represents an outmoded past. If a new epoch is truly to emerge it will begin with new thought, new patterns of world relationships, and what Richard Falk calls an "ethic of global concern." The choice is whether the planet earth belongs to all the peoples of the world or whether some people have special claims on the earth's resources at the expense of others.

4.

The future of America depends on. . .

LEARNING A LESSON FROM THE VIETNAM WAR

It is not in our interests to deal with the West, which represents the present not the future. In ten year's time there will probably be in Thailand, which always responds to the dominant wind, a pro-Chinese neutralist government and South Vietnam will certainly be governed by Ho Chi Minh or his successor. Our interests are served by dealing with the camp that one day will dominate the whole of Asia—and by coming to terms before its victory—in order to obtain the best terms possible.—Prince Norodin Sihanouk of Cambodia, 1964.

At the very time the United States began its bicentennial celebrations, the war in Indochina ground to a halt. Cambodia fell to the insurgent Khmer Rouge. South Vietnam was taken over by the Viet Cong and the Democratic Republic of Vietnam; the Laotian coalition government collapsed to become dominated by the Pathet Lao. Each of these groups were nationalis-

49

tic, anti-Western, and to one degree or another Marxist in ideology.

This marked the end of a war that had been going on for more than thirty years. First it was directed against the French, then the Japanese, again against the French, and finally the Americans. American involvement began in the early 1950s but intensified in 1962–63 with the widespread use of military advisors to the South Vietnamese army.

The twelve-year American involvement was the longest war in American history. More than 52,000 Americans lost their lives and over 300,000 were wounded in Indochina. The number of Cambodians and Vietnamese killed will never be known. Deaths certainly totaled over 1 million, with triple that number wounded and the total refugees in the three countries approaching half the total population.

The twelve-year conflict was the most divisive force in American politics since the Civil War. The impact of the war on the culture and mentality of the American people is incalculable. Terms like Vietnamization, My Lai, and gook are now commonplace. Smart bombs, antipersonnel mines, and napalm have become established forms of warfare. Six million Vietnam veterans and 100,000 Vietnamese refugees in the United States will insure that the war is not soon forgotten.

We need not repeat the details of the collapse of South Vietnam and the triumph of the Khmer Rouge. It is necessary, however, to seek some explanations—not because the answers are obvious but rather because President Ford and the Pentagon are suggesting explanations that simply don't explain, if they are not downright untrue.

It would not be correct to say President Ford has expressed a comprehensive or definitive opinion. He and his secretaries of state and defense, however, have suggested a line of thought which says the United States, especially the Congress, lost Indochina.

The executive office interpretation rests on the assumption that South Vietnam and Cambodia were invaded by an outside power motivated by an alien ideology—communism. These alien forces subverted a free and open society and ultimately triumphed through superior military power. The final victory came, as President Ford described it, because "the United States did not carry out its commitment in the supplying of military hardware and economic aid." Indeed, Ford went so far as to tell CBS newsmen that the South Vietnamese army would not have retreated if Congress had appropriated the funds requested by the administration.

This mythology without doubt is being widely accepted in the United States. It is the same mythology used in the early 1950s to explain who lost China, it is a myth that assumes the United States controls Asian geography, that the revolutionary forces in Asia run counter to American and Western interests, that the governments of Presidents Lon Nol and Thieu were democratic and that Indochina society was free and open.

The facts, not the myths, are substantially the opposite. Neither the United States nor the Congress nor the Democrats lost Indochina. The developments in Southeast Asia were set in motion long ago by the peoples themselves. Only now has the United States, for a variety of reasons, mostly as a result of the anti-war movement, begun to realize what kind of society and government the Vietnamese and Cambodians want for themselves.

Harold Isaacs, a distinguished student of Asia, wrote in 1950, when President Truman recognized Bao Dai as the ruler of Vietnam rather than Ho Chi Minh, that "with [this act] the United States embarked upon another ill-conceived adventure doomed to end in self-inflicted defeat. The real problem," he noted, "is not how to implement this policy but how to extricate ourselves from it."

Isaacs sensed that what President Sihanouk understood, as quoted at the beginning of this chapter—that the West in Asia "represents the present not the future." Sihanouk in 1964 understood that the revolutionary forces were a potent fusion of communism and nationalism striving to modernize traditional societies. Sihanouk also recognized that Bao Dai, Diem, Ky, Thieu, and their kind were the remnants of a feudal oligarchy held in power as the puppets of an alien power—first the French and later the United States. The future, however, lay with the persons who understood the Vietnamese proverb which says, "The law of the emperor yields to the custom of the village." For thirty years French and American colonial power prevented the law of the emperor from yielding.

Indeed the collapse of South Vietnam appears now

not to be so much the result of military power but rather a massive recognition that the revolutionaries are indeed meant to rule. Some fled and others will fail to adjust, but most Vietnamese long ago were prepared to accept Ho Chi Minh and the Viet Minh as the ruling party and ideology of their country. These revolutionary leaders are Communists, to be sure, but also Vietnamese not encumbered with the heritage of exploitation associated with colonial powers like France and the United States.

The United States may have lost Indochina. If it lost, however, it was because the United States identified with forces of reaction, dependence, and corruption. The vision of a new society, authentically indigenous, belonged to Hanoi and the Provisional Revolutionary Government. Ho Chi Minh, not Diem and Thieu, was known as the George Washington of Vietnam. It was the revolutionaries, not the warlords of the south, who imitated the Declaration of Independence.

The point is that the United States never had a right to consider Vietnam as its territory. The war in Indochina was a civil war between forces of the future and forces of the past. The United States backed the wrong horse. Congress, in not voting more funds for South Vietnam, simply recognized what more and more Americans recognized and what the Vietnamese decided long ago—Thieu did not have a popular mandate to rule.

This is not to say that North Vietnam, the Khmer Rouge, or the Provisional Revolutionary Government are ideal or even good structures. They have fostered too much violence and fomented too much disarray.

They are, however, the authentic nationalists of the Indochina peninsula.

The real issue is not why the United States lost Indochina, but rather why the United States backed the wrong side. Why did the United States support the forces of reaction and corruption rather than the forces of nationalism and modernization?

Answering this question will preoccupy historians and analysts for years to come. But there are several clues. One is that after World War II the United States moved into a power vacuum left by the collapse of the British and French empires. Another is the fear of communism that has pervaded American policy makers from the 1920s to the present. In fighting the cold war, United States power moved wherever and whenever it could to thwart what were thought to be Russian or Chinese initiatives.

These understandable reasons, however, don't explain how a nation long known as a liberal democracy and advocate of national independence and free societies could become so enmeshed with the forces of yesterday, rather than identifying with the vanguard of tomorrow. Or have Americans misperceived who they are and their own objectives in the world?

Perhaps unknown to ourselves the forces of history have changed the character of the United States from a republic of free people into an imperial machine whose main concern is the preservation of its status and power. Perhaps our concerns have shifted from freedom and the promotion of independence to a passion for security and the protection of our surpluses. If this is the case, the end of the Indochina war should be an occasion not to lament the loss of imperial power but to reform the American body politic so that there will be no more Vietnams.

5.

The future of America depends on. . .

RESOLVING CONFLICT PEACEFULLY

What characterizes our time . . . is the way the masses and their wretched condition have burst upon contemporary sensibilities. . . . The masses have become stronger and keep people from forgetting them.—Albert Camus.

During the spring of 1975 when President Gerald Ford officially opened bicentennial celebrations, he also declared, "The war is over." He referred to the end of more than twelve years of massive military involvement in Indochina. Although most Americans would welcome a new era of peace, it is doubtful, given the human situation, that the violence of recent years will be greatly diminished.

Historian C.E. Black says, "The modern age, more than any other, has been an age of assassinations, of civil, religious, and international wars, of mass slaughter in many forms, and of concentration camps. Never before has human life been disposed of so lightly as the price for immediate goals."

When conflict and violence shift to the Third World, as was the case with Vietnam, it becomes easy to forget that Western culture has a history of crimes as spectacular as its technological successes. In the twentieth century alone consider the 10 million deaths of World War I, the brutalities of revolutionary Russia, the extermination of 6 million Jews in Nazi death camps, the 20 millions more who died on the battlefields or in the bombings of Hamburg, Kassel, Dresden, Tokyo, Hiroshima, and Nagasaki during World War II. Franz Fanon speaks for many Third World peoples in his indictment of European man whom he says is "only a succession of negations of man, and an avalanche of murders."

We live in what Raymond Aaron calls *The Century of Total War*. What had been essentially a European pastime before 1950 has now become a global activity. One reason for the prevalence of war has been the triumph of politics. Where before man had a series of allegiances and alternative routes to achieve his goals—religious, economic, cultural, artistic—now "politics is everything" and the processes of politics prevail. When older traditions of ethics disappear, all that is left is the cult of power. This in its extreme is total war, described by the former Nazi Albert Speer as "all available means of violence, treachery, and terror as applied without scruples."

We see enough conflict on television and in the press to be aware of the pervasiveness of confrontation politics. Perhaps we are becoming insensitive to the size and intensity of the problem. Some years ago Secretary of Defense Robert McNamara said there were "149 serious internal insurgencies" during the decade preceding 1965. A more recent estimate reports that since 1945 the world has experienced 15 limited wars, over 50 coup d'etats, more than 75 rebellions for independence, and approximately 200 social revolutions—not to mention racial, religious, and nationality riots. During these years the United States has engaged in 8 major wars and over 100 military actions.

The major conflagrations of recent years outside North America include big international conflicts in Indochina and the Middle East, civil wars in Pakistan, Northern Ireland, Nigeria, Chad, Sudan, and Portuguese Africa, insurgencies in Thailand, the Philippines, Uruguay, Guatamala, and South Africa. No one knows how many lives have been wasted, how many innocents have suffered, how much wealth has been consumed or diverted, or how deep the hostilities have been driven to plant seeds for further conflict. What we must never forget is that wherever there is injustice, wherever man's inhumanity to man is perpetrated or ignored, conflict has spilled over into violence.

Nor are there prospects that conflict and violence will be any less frequent and devastating in the future. C.E. Black says, "It is more likely that there will be ten to fifteen revolutions a year for the foreseeable future in the less developed societies in addition to the many forms of domestic strife in the societies that are more developed." He believes "the loss of life due to violence is significantly greater in proportion to population in modern than in traditional societies." Based on the abysmal record of the past, Black poses the hard reality:

The Christian peoples have certainly been among the most ruthless in their treatment of one another and of peoples of other faiths, and the greatest wars of modern times have been generated within the orbit of their influence, but it remains to be seen whether the peoples of other faiths will be more humane when they face the hard choices posed by modernization.

Certain givens foreshadow more conflict. One of these is the fundamental human predicament. Evil and depravity rest right in the middle of events. Another given is power. Persons and institutions with power seek to use it to their own advantage. Those without it seek power to control their destiny. The many elements constituting power are dynamic and in constant flux.

Another given is people, individually and collectively. No conflict erupts apart from people. But there is instability here as well. The character of people changes along with their interests and desires. In the past, considerable conflict developed from the movement of people from one region to another. Today the greatest source of instability is not migration but internal growth. The doubling and tripling of population in certain areas within a decade creates frightful consequences. The disintegration of Calcutta, for instance, is partially the result of a population which soared from 1.5 million in 1940 to 5 million in 1970 with an expected 20 million by the year 2000. This growth, apart from any other social needs, is fertile soil for violence and upheaval. The urbanization of the villager is another of the potent sources of disturbance today, especially when vast numbers of city dwellers are permanently unemployed.

Another given in conflict is change. The transition from one status to another always involves tension between the new and the old. Today this tension is magnified by the rapidity and magnitude of social change so that the underpinnings of stability no longer exist.

Simply reflect on the trauma of parents living in an isolated African village whose children are graduating from the University of London. Multiply this millions of times and you begin to sense the tension that accompanies the leap from traditional society to the Atomic Age in one generation. George Kennan's comment in this regard is worth pondering.

> Wherever the ... experience of the father becomes irrelevant to the trials and searchings of the son—there the foundations of man's inner health and stability begin to crumble. ... These are the marks of an era of rapid technological and social change ... and if the price is to cut man's ties to the past and catapult him violently across centuries of adjustment into some new and unfamiliar technological stratosphere, then I am not sure the achievement is worth it.

When one thinks of conflict, the most conspicuous form that springs to mind is aggressive war. What is significant is that the traditional attack of one power on another (Germany on Poland or the United States on Spain) does not seem to be widely engaged in at this moment. Some such conflicts continue between Russia and China, India and Pakistan, Israel and her neighbors, and not long ago between San Salvador and Honduras. Perhaps the Soviet/American cold war, with its strategies of expansion and containment, continues to be a variant of great power rivalry. But such conflicts are presently superceded by conflicts *within* states rather than *between* states.

Most of the conflicts in modern societies, at least since World War II, are civil wars or insurgencies. These are struggles by various political groups to seize power and exercise it on their own terms. Occasionally outside powers become directly involved in such civil wars. More often they play a dominant role within the state through political or economic domination. The issues at stake are largely indigenous in nature. The principal issue is usually not national security but rather the making of a nation. Often such insurgency is not characterized by open confrontation but rather by the hit-and-run tactics of an underground guerrilla force.

But the important considerations are what creates insurgencies and why we can expect more of them. In a nutshell, the cause of most contemporary conflict is the revolutionary struggle for liberation from political domination, economic enslavement, and cultural impoverishment. Various routes are followed, numerous slogans describe the process, but the goal is to lift the burden so well described by Chekhov a century ago.

During the summer and the winter there had been hours and days when it seemed as if these people [the peasants] lived worse than cattle, and it was terrible to be with them. They were coarse, dishonest, dirty, and drunken; they did not live at peace with one another but quarreled continually, because they feared, suspected, and despised one another. . . . Crushing labor that made the whole body ache at night, cruel winters, scanty crops, overcrowding, and no help, and nowhere to look for help.

The goal of each liberation movement as Richard Barnet puts it, is a "radical redistribution of political and economic power to overcome the centuries of political oppression and crushing poverty." This involves creating the essence of nationhood—a national self-consciousness. It means breaking the apathy, fatalism, superstition, and distrust of the traditional society. It calls for overthrowing obsolete institutions and reactionary leadership.

Liberation means freedom from outside political and economic control. Today increasingly the attack is on "neo-imperialism"—economic exploitation by developed nations in collaboration with a local privileged class. Liberation means death to ideologies of racial and cultural superiority. Liberation means the possibility of exercising one's power in such a way as to determine one's own destiny. John A. Hannah, chief administrator of the Agency for International Development (AID) has caught the spirit of liberation when he observes, "We live in a world at a time when it is no longer believed by people in the poor nations that God has ordained that people should grow up in hunger, disease, and ignorance."

The road to liberation is never complete. Alan Brash

in this regard says, "Development is that which contributes to social justice, self-reliance, and economic growth—in that order of priority." This being the case, no society has as yet arrived (although some have charted the course) at economic prosperity and political power, now the goal of all peoples.

The process of development or satisfying "rising expectations" is called modernization. A new political system means the overthrow of the old and competition between the new alternatives—communist or capitalist, authoritarian or democratic. A new economic structure means reorienting the economy from agriculture to industry, new forms of investment, and the discarding of inhibiting ideas and structures. Modernization includes intellectual, social, psychological, and religious changes as well.

At each step of the way modernization has been accompanied by the greatest calamities mankind has known. The new way of life inevitably involves the transformation of the traditional way of life. And in this complex of changes conflict and violence are inevitable. Only a few countries such as Canada and Australia have been able to modernize without extensive violence. But even here the price has been heavy for the Indian and the bushman. Robert Heilbronner reflects on the pain and price of modernization by comparing it to the violence of the status quo.

I do not know how one measures the moral price of historical victories or how one can ever decide that a diffuse gain is worth a sharp and particular loss. I only know that the way in which we ordinarily keep the books of history is wrong. No one is now toting up the balance of the wretches who starve in India, or the peasants of Northeastern Brazil who lived in the swamps on crabs, or the undernourished and permanently stunted children of Hong Kong or Honduras. Their sufferings go unrecorded, and are not present to counterbalance the scales when the furies of revolution strike down their victims. Barrington Moore has made a nice calculation that bears on this problem. Taking as the weight in one pan the 35,000 to 40,000 persons who lost their lives—mainly for no fault of theirs—as a result of the terror during the French Revolution, he asks what would have been the death rate from preventable starvation and injustice under the *ancien regime* to balance the scales. "Offhand," he writes, "it seems unlikely that this would be very much below the proportion of .0010 which [the] figure of 40,000 yields when set against an estimated population of 24 million."

Is it unjust to charge the *ancien regime* in Russia with 10 million preventable deaths? I think it not unreasonable. To charge the authorities in pre-revolutionary China with equally vast and preventable degradations? Theodore White, writing in 1946, had this to say: ". . . some scholars think that China is perhaps the only country in the world where the people eat less, live more bitterly, and are clothed worse than they were five hundred years ago."

Whatever conflict situation one discusses these days, be it South Africa, Angola-Portugal, the Middle East, or Indochina, the operative myth is liberation, the process modernization. The extent of the change contemplated is so great, the transformation so complete we label such events revolution. For many twentieth-century people the aspiration for liberation and modernization is as revolutionary as the process itself. The cliché "revolutionary world" focuses on the fact of all-embracing change and the realization that never before have so many crucial developments reached fulfillment all at once.

Before leaving this description of conflict, we ought to observe in passing that the problem we are discussing does have international ramifications. On the one hand, the great powers, especially the United States, Russia, and the Western European states are deeply implicated in the structures of life in these conflict situations. Much of the wealth desperately needed in the less developed world finally accrues to investors in the rich lands. Trading patterns put countries dependent on the sale of raw materials in debt to the industrial powers. Add to this the blinding inheritance of racism which was used to excuse centuries of exploitation.

It is hard for us to imagine the depths of resentment that currently inspire so many Third World peoples. These grow out of their profound attempt to escape dependency and to determine their own destiny. The deep despair is compounded by the recent discovery on the part of some groups that they are peoples no longer integral in the total world economy. Economist Nathan

Keyfitz suggests that countries previously important for their raw materials have now been superseded by synthetics. "Worse than exploited," he says, "they are irrelevant." Peoples in this situation turn to violence not as a means to an end but as an act through which they gain identity.

Fanon observes that violence in such circumstances "frees the native from his inferiority complex and from his despair and inaction; it makes him fearless and restores his self-respect." Ronald Segal adds, "What the world, therefore, has to face is a despair so deep among the poor, a resentment against established conditions so passionate that normal fears are ceasing to exercise their expected restraint." Perhaps this explains the persistent power of the Vietnamese against the greatest concentration of destructive power ever amassed in such a small area. Segal applies such feeling to the entire world where he says we face a "final accommodation of an equal humanity or an equal annihilation."

The realities of world hunger mean that today more human lives are at stake than were lost in all the wars of world history. Betty Cabezas of the Latin American Center for Economic and Social Development observed in 1969 that between 270 million and 300 million Latin Americans will, in 30 years, be marginal to the economy. She observed that this spread across several generations could lead to a deterioration of humanity and evolving mutation where substantial groups of people will become "by the end of the century, the primitives of the civilized; and in the next century, the apes of the new humanity."

The nature of power is to defend itself. As Americans we find ourselves defending the status quo and protecting our investments throughout the world. Though aggression is out of fashion, the United States has found itself involved in Vietnam, Lebanon, the Dominican Republic, Guatamala, and Greece, defending corrupt and backward oligarchies, holding back the movements for liberation. Counterinsurgency has become the primary preoccupation of United States military planners.

To distinguish between acceptable and nonacceptable conflict is no easy task. In the international sphere and to a great degree in domestic affairs, power is the basis of legitimacy. For most North Americans violence in behalf of the established order or status quo is judged by one set of criteria, insurgent violence by another. Protestor violence is roundly condemned. Police excesses are excusable. Because of this dilemma, but more fundamentally because of what violence does, some observers refuse to distinguish between types of violence. Jacques Ellul, for one, says "violence is of a piece" from the competition of the marketplace to the war to defend the fatherland. All violence, all conflict, Ellul says, "is the form that human relations normally and necessarily take apart from Christ."

The first task for the North American Christian is to reckon with the conflict within our own culture—black and brown versus white, rich versus poor, urban versus rural, French versus English. These conflicts are also part of our church life. There will be little redemptive witness on our part overseas unless we are a reconciled and reconciling community here. Absalom Vilakazi, speaking for the church in Africa, says that "Africans measure the sincerity of American missionary or Christian activity by the way American churches accept or reject the Negro in their midst."

We need to search out those ways we have been and are part of conflict situations. On the one hand, we are learning how conflict and violence is a product of good people who refuse to be responsible. Marjorie Hope says the "violence we recognize least is the violence of indifference." Brazilian Archbishop Helder Camera lectures on how "Christians rob Christians." What they mean is the apathy of the church in the face of catastrophe and the involvement of the church in the processes of exploitation.

Jesus one time lamented over the people of Jerusalem, "Would that even today you knew the things that make for peace!" If we are truly going to work for peace, we will need to work on the many ramifications of our involvement in conflict. Alan Brash cited one such example in an address on "American Christians in World Development." The action of many churches to assume responsibility for their investments in corporations working in Portuguese Africa and South Africa, he reported, has had a profound effect on the church in Africa. It means a great deal to the African church when American churches begin to exercise their investment power for racial and economic justice.

One thing Jesus certainly meant in his lament was that the people of Jerusalem had cheapened the meaning of the term peace. Peace, for Jesus included all the richness of the Hebrew *Shalom*. Not simply an absence of conflict but a relationship that included justice, welfare, and prosperity for all. In a similar way the concept of peace has been cheapened in our time. Some politicize peace, others internalize peace.

For the Christian there is no peace where there is injustice or exploitation. The only way to resolve conflict and violence for the Christian is to create right relationships, domestically and internationally, based on institutions which will be conducive to a just economic and social order.

6.

The future of America depends on. . .

KEEPING OUR GOVERNMENT HONEST

The true crime of Richard Nixon was simple: he destroyed the myth that binds America together—Theodore H. White.

One of the ironies of American history is that the bicentennial and centennial observances have come at the low point of the nation's political life. Most historians rank the Grant administration of 1869–77 as the most corrupt in American history. Grant, however, finished his two terms in office. Now in the 1970s, we have endured another spectacle of political failure, including the resignations of both a President and a Vice-President. Watergate, an apartment complex in Washington, D.C., has become a metaphor for a complex series of political shenanigans that shattered the legitimacy of a government.

The things now collectively called Watergate include the following:

1. An act of political espionage when representatives of the new Committee to Reelect the President bugged and burglarized the Democratic headquarters located in an office building complex known as Watergate.

2. A systematic attempt by White House officials to cover up their involvement in this espionage.

3. The lying, deception, and perjury of government officials who tried to avoid being implicated in the conspiracy.

4. Violation of the campaign spending laws by failing to report some 2 million dollars given to the Committee to Reelect the President. Most of these funds were held in private bank accounts and vaults to avoid public knowledge of their existence and use.

5. Spending campaign money to buy influence to prevent the Security and Exchange Commission investigation into the financial empire of Robert Vesco.

6. The deliberate (and successful) forgery of letters to sabotage the presidential primary campaign of Senator Muskie, plus attempted forged cables to implicate President Kennedy in the assassination of President Diem of Vietnam in 1963.

7. The use of official government investigative agencies—the FBI and CIA—in interparty rivalry and the cover-up of criminal affairs.

8. A series of wiretaps ordered by the President in 1969–71 on persons connected with the National Security Council, presumably for national security reasons, such as to hide the bombing of Cambodia and Laos.

9. Destruction of documents and failure to keep proper records of official governmental and campaign activities and funding.

10. A mentality so generated by the fear of losing an election or jeopardizing national security that the law

was used by officials for their own purposes regardless of its ultimate effect on the nation.

11. The refusal of the executive branch of the government to supply information regarding the criminal behavior of certain officials; and the invoking of presidential privilege to prevent public scrutiny of policy and its implementation.

12. A political style which views its opposition as enemies to be destroyed rather than a loyal minority with constitutional rights of their own.

13. Taping official conversations and revelations of the cryptic and frequently obscene language used in the White House.

14. The use of political power and influence by Vice President Agnew for personal gain and more comfortable living.

15. Interference with the freedom of Special Prosecutor Archibald Cox to complete his inquiry.

16. Congressional committees—Senate Select and House Judiciary—which investigated, held hearings, and finally voted to recommend impeachment of President Nixon.

The climax of Watergate was the second time in six years that an American President was forced to abdicate. Lyndon Johnson in April 1968, decided he could not win reelection without a serious struggle and retired at the end of his term in January 1969. His successor, Richard Nixon, was the first President to resign his office when impeachment and conviction became virtually inevitable.

"Our Constitution works." This strong phrase from President Ford's inaugural emphasizes the legality and constitutional framework of these events. Many Americans have been impatient during these past years as the evidence of presidential wrongdoing accumulated. This should not be surprising, for the wheels of constitutional democracy do move slowly. Where individual rights are cherished and the rule of law is respected, hasty action may be more harmful than deliberate movement.

Every President takes an oath of office to "preserve, protect, and defend the Constitution of the United States." One of his constitutional obligations is to see "that the laws are faithfully executed." Every President knows that he can be removed from office if impeached and convicted of "treason, bribery, or other high crimes and misdemeanors."

It may be trite to point out that the attempt to burglarize the Democratic National Committee headquarters in the Watergate on June 16, 1972, was a criminal offense. From this illegality, sponsored by the Committee to Reelect the President, came a mountain of subsequent crimes in the twenty-four months of cover-up, some of which continue to the present.

Forcing President Nixon to leave office was legal and constitutional in every way. First, the grand jury indicted those caught at the break-in. Then came trial in the United States District Court of Judge John Sirica in Washington, D.C. At the sentencing of James McCord the evidence of White House involvement in the burglary came out. Following this the United States Senate Committee under Senator Sam Ervin conducted public hearings. More evidence. A special prosecutor was appointed to look into the Watergate break-in and cover-up. Finally the House of Representatives ordered its Judiciary Committee to begin an inquiry into whether President Nixon should be impeached.

The Judiciary Committee, under the leadership of Chairman Peter Rodino and Special Counsel John Doar and Albert E. Jenner, Jr., reviewed the evidence and conducted public hearings. The committee majority decided the President was indeed guilty, and voted three articles of impeachment.

The system worked. Because of dutiful policemen, the burglars were apprehended. Because of freedom of the press, the *Washington Post* was able to expose the cover-up. (Read Woodward and Bernstein's *All the President's Men* for a masterful account of enterprising reporters and a courageous newspaper.) Because of the separation of powers, independent-minded judges performed their duties faithfully. Because of a concerned public, special prosecutors were appointed. Because of a passion for the law, the Judiciary Committee embarked upon the distasteful task of removing the President. Because the wrongdoing was so evident and obvious, the Congress, led by members of the President's own Republican party, informed the President he would have to leave office voluntarily or involuntarily,

The new President rightfully said, "Our Constitution works. Our great republic is a government of laws and not of men."

What should not be forgotten is that Richard Nixon was not only a villain but also a victim. He simply acted the way American Presidents have been conducting themselves for the past generation.

"The question which concerns me most about this new administration is whether it lacks a genuine sense of conviction about what is right and what is wrong." This question is not from the administration of Richard Nixon or Lyndon Johnson, where it would have been most appropriate. This statement by Chester Bowles in 1961 reflects his concern about the administration of John Kennedy. It could have been raised about earlier administrations, but the point now is that governments in Washington have been lacking in moral judgment for quite a while.

In many respects the Nixon resignation was the result of fourteen years of power exercised by Presidents increasingly out of touch with the people and increasingly independent of the other branches of government.

One of the main reasons for presidential government instead of congressional government or a balanced democratic government is the powerful defense establishment, recurring wars, threat of wars, and the imperial domination of peoples who are not American. The military mentality emphasizes preparedness, politics as conflict between friends and enemies instead of party differences, simplicity in analysis, and speed in resolving problems. Above all the military mind justifies its actions on the basis of national security.

John Kennedy represented this perspective in his inaugural address: "Ask not what your country can do for you; ask what you can do for your country." Richard Nixon, right up to his farewell address, used the same argument. He said there were some mistakes during his administration, but "they were made in what

I believed at the time to be the best interest of the nation."

Precisely this kind of thinking made possible what Arthur Schlesinger calls "The Imperial Presidency." Schlesinger is not commenting on the Nixon propensity for the pomp, glitter, and homage of an imperial potentate. Rather, the imperial president rules instead of represents; he dominates the legislative and judicial branches of the government. Many observers consider the American President to have more personal, unencumbered power than Brezhnev and Kosygin in the Kremlin. The balance of powers established in the Constitution has tilted dangerously in favor of the President. "The Imperial Presidency" must be curbed. Perhaps Watergate will help bring the presidency into proper balance with the other branches of government.

One of the major preoccupations of the Judiciary Committee as they debated the President's fate was the impact of their action on the institution of the presidency. Many committee members argued that if Congress failed to act at this point, Congress would become a perpetually inferior partner in the government. Subsequent impeachments would be impossible. Other members pondered an impeachment's effect on the character of the presidency. Fortunately, the committee allowed the Constitution to supercede partisanship and the law to apply even to Presidents.

The real issue raised by Watergate, and indeed the Vietnam War which was waged without a congressional declaration, is the question of legitimacy.

The Constitution of the United States assumes a government created by the people for certain specific functions, a government whose legitimacy rests on its accountability to the people and their Constitution. The Declaration of Independence and the Constitution assume that political legitimacy concerns how political power is established and how such power is used. "Incumbency in itself," as Protestant Attorney William Stringfellow puts it, "is not enough to validate any exercise of political authority."

Watergate and the Agnew affair brought the question of legitimacy to the forefront. We heard it dozens of times as politicians and commentators emphasized that the country was being torn apart or that the country could not endure the continuing exposés of corruption and violation of constitutional principles. Vice-President Agnew reportedly resigned not because he felt he did anything wrong, but because if he had remained in office or vindicated himself through the Congress and the courts, "it would have meant subjecting the country to a further agonizing period of months without an unclouded succession to the presidency. . . . The American people deserve to have a Vice-President who commands their unimpaired confidence and implicit trust." Something is troublesome about this point of view. If we are a society and government based on law, then it should not be unduly traumatic if the prerogatives of the law are exercised and lawbreakers are prosecuted justly and mercifully.

Then Attorney General Richardson argued on the basis of legitimacy that Agnew had to resign and his corruption be exposed "in order to achieve and enhance the public confidence in our institutions and the administration of justice. I would hope," he added, "that most fundamentally all of us would have confidence that our system works." Mr. Richardson later put it eloquently when he said he believed he could better serve his country by resigning than by continuing in office.

The resignation of President Nixon and Vice-President Agnew did not resolve the issue of legitimacy. Revelations regarding CIA activities in Chile and Greece suggest responsible units of the government continue to act illegally. Wiretapping, assassination squads, illegal opening of mail (even the President's), to name only a few of the obvious infractions, illustrate that the questions of illegitimacy are not limited to the executive department or simply to personal weaknesses. A government which is prepared to subvert legitimately constituted governments abroad will not fear to subvert constitutional structures at home.

There are yet other reasons why the American populate question the legitimacy not only of the Nixon administration, but of the government itself. Throughout the sixties the oppressed minorities asked whether the government indeed "established justice, insured domestic tranquility, and promoted the general welfare."

Others asked what government can be legitimate that not only wages war apart from constitutional procedures but carries on such warfare against traditionally armed people with the grotesque weaponry of technological man. The fourteen months of secret bombing of Cambodia before the formal invasion in 1970 compounds the constitutional and moral question. Quaker economist Kenneth Boulding asks whether the national state itself can be considered legitimate. Whenever a "government cannot do anything for me," he says, "it has lost its legitimacy" and must be transformed or abandoned. "As the present system contains a positive probability of nuclear war, it is in fact bankrupt and should be changed before the nuclear war rather than afterward." The MAD situation of "mutually assured destruction" whether in the Middle East or the entire world is a result of governments no longer existing for the general welfare. President Nixon's frequent contention that the United States must play "a major role" in the world "because there is no one else to play it," that "the hope of the world for peace ... rests in America" represents an illegitimate political arrogance and a world view no longer acceptable as part of the regular moral or social order within which we live.

Because of Watergate, Agnew, the Southeast Asia bombing, and the continuing failure of the American government to insure the rights of all its citizens, the American people are dangerously close to no longer trusting their rulers.

Kenneth Boulding observed, "It is precisely at the moment of apparent invincibility that an institution is in gravest danger." This has certainly been true during these traumatic years. There are some good omens that the system is making some necessary adjustment. Congress has passed legislation curbing the war-making powers of the President. The Department of Justice has seized the initiative to purify the ranks of the corrupt and to prosecute the abusers of power. The courts have in every case freed those who were prosecuted in Gainsville, Harrisburg, Los Angeles, and New York, who in their eagerness to challenge the illegitimate actions of the government ran afoul of the old regime. Congress forced an end to American intervention in Southeast Asia. Curbing the power of the Presidency appears as the beginning of trust in the sytems.

The main concerns of those who designed the Constitution of the United States was to insure a government of laws. This included checks and balances, openness and public responsibility. There is no more important bicentennial project than the restoration of legitimacy to the American government.

7.

The future of America depends on. . .

DETERMINING WHO IS OUR GOD: UNCLE SAM OR JESUS?

Let us beware of the real danger of misplaced allegiance, if not outright idolatry, to the extent that we fail to distinguish between the god of an American civil religion, and the God who reveals himself in the holy Scriptures and in Jesus Christ.

If we as leaders appeal to the god of civil religion, our faith is in a small and exclusive deity, a loyal spiritual advisor, the object of a national folk religion devoid of moral conduct. But if we pray to the biblical God of justice and righteousness, we fall under God's judgment for calling upon his name but failing to obey his commands.—Senator Mark O. Hatfield

One of the most provocative concepts for understanding American culture and politics has been the term "civil religion." Though a term derived from the eighteenth-century French philosopher Rousseau, Robert Bellah, a sociologist of religion, popularized the concept in a 1966 article describing it as an important ingredient in both American politics and religion.

Bellah's insight was not particularly new or unique. Yet the notion of civil religion, the intermeshing of the civil and religious orders is striking because it contradicts one of the most cherished concepts of the American political and religious thought—the separation of church and state. Though there have been frequent court tests of this assumption, both political theory and religious thought justify and promote the idea and practice of separation.

For our purposes we will accept the observation that all peoples, perhaps all individuals, are religious in some form or other. People tend to have faith in god, some power outside themselves. They have feelings of awe and reverence. They participate in rites and ceremonies. Some religions are very simple and personal. The major world religions have complex systems of thought and patterns of belief.

Americans tend to be a highly religious people, at least when compared to Europeans or even Latin Americans. Some 50 percent of the population are church members. An even higher percentage believe in the existence of a deity and will at times pray to Him.

The Bible reports severe differences between religions. In the Old Testament sharp clashes occurred repeatedly between the followers of Yahweh and the Canaanite faith of Baalism. Later differences divided the faithful remnant and the apostate majority within Judaism. The early church, following the teachings of Jesus, separated itself from the Jews. Christians have splintered into many subgroupings.

Obviously there are many religions, many faiths. Yet these faiths serve similar purposes. Most religions are or become essential ingredients in organizing and integrating society. For this reason minority faiths are frequently limited in their influence and impact. Some sociologists say every functioning society has to have a common religion.

It is beyond our scope to point out the uniqueness of the Christian faith. Suffice it to say that one generalization that distinguishes the gospel is the belief that "God was in Christ reconciling the world." The Bible describes how God came to man, not how man in his searching found God. "In short," William Stringfellow says, "religion supposes that God is yet to be discovered; Christianity knows that God has already come among us." The church is a community of people, the Apostle Paul tells us, which supercedes cultural, linguistic, and political boundaries. (See Galatians 3:28.)

Neither can we describe in detail the vast differences between varieties of Christians. It is possible to distinguish between those Christians who followed the lead of the Roman Emperor Constantine to make Christianity an integral part of sociopolitical order and the small minorities who throughout the ages believed that the organic unity of church, government, and society represented the fall of the church. The free churches, the medieval sectarians, the Anabaptists and Mennonites, English Baptists, and Latin American Pentecostals tenaciously believed that Christ would always be subverted when allied with political power.

The vast majority of Europeans who settled the Atlantic seaboard in the seventeenth and eighteenth centuries followed the Constantinian alliance of church and state. The New England Puritans proposed a new Israel which would not be guilty of the sins of either the old Israel or of Europe. The colonial settlements were seen as the beginning of a new Christian civilization. Church historian Robert Handy says that the major denominations, as recently as the early twentieth century, "thought of themselves as composing the religious mainstream of the nation ... especially charged with making America a Christian nation."

Hence when sectarians came to New England they were severely persecuted. Roman Catholics were unwanted in nearly every colony except Maryland. Jews were ostracized. Fortunately, the Pennsylvania experiment of religious liberty and the secular critics of the eighteenth century were influential enough to win religious toleration for all groups. But the idea of a Protestant nation waned very slowly; indeed some persons today continue to press for Protestant principles disregarding the presence of 50 million Roman Catholics and 6 million Jews.

During the nineteenth and early twentieth century not only did Protestantism cease to be the majority faith but Protestants, like most Christians, became increasingly secularized. Part of this process was to identify less and less as Protestants and more and more as Americans.

Every nation develops a mythology of its own. America is no exception. The American revolution provided patron saints in the Founding Fathers and major statements of faith in the Declaration of Independence and the Constitution. Wars produced heroes and a sense of tragedy. National holidays became times to sing songs in praise of the nation and to make speeches extolling national purpose. Often these ceremonies invoked the name of God and borrowed freely from the ideas of the Christian tradition. New immigrants to the United States were Americanized to think like the residents already here. Sidney Mead observed that American Protestantism became Americanism by the early twentieth century: "Under the system of official separation of church and state the denominations eventually found themselves as completely identified with nationalism and their country's political and economic system as had ever been known in Christendom."

Civil religion can only be understood in context—the role of religion in society, the Constantinian tradition in the church, the search for a Protestant America, and the rise of American nationalism. The term itself is from Rousseau who in *The Social Contract* believed "there is therefore a purely civil profession of faith of which the Sovereign should fix the articles, not exactly as religious dogmas but as social sentiments without which a man cannot be a good citizen or a faithful subject." In spite of his hostility to traditional Christianity, Rousseau borrowed freely from his understanding of the roles of Christianity as dispenser of dogma and as integrater of society and culture.

The more recent use of the term "civil religion," beginning with sociologist Robert Bellah, suggests that the American political realm has a religious dimension—a set of beliefs, symbols, and rituals. This civil religion is focused on such relatively recent terminology as "In God we trust" and "This nation under God" but its roots go back to the terminology of the Declaration of Independence—Supreme Judge, Divine Providence, Creator, and nature's God.

Bellah says this civil religion existed alongside Christianity through most of American history. It supplied "an understanding of the American experience in the light of ultimate and universal reality." Though it borrowed heavily from Christianity, Bellah thinks it has not become a substitute for the real thing.

One of the characteristics of all religious experiences is to borrow ideas and insights from surrounding faiths and cultures. Some of this is necessary and wholesome. But the danger is that indiscriminate borrowing will create a new synthesis, a syncretism which is so different it no longer resembles the authentic faith it purports to be.

Civil religion in the United States was never pure. It always partook of Christian elements. The real tragedy, however, is that the church in the United States borrowed so freely from the civil religion and national mythology that Christianity for many persons became indistinguishable from Americanism.

Will Herberg, the distinguished Jewish sociologist, says that Americans by and large have a common religion, "the American Way of Life." This he says is "a spiritual structure, a structure of ideas and ideals, of aspirations and values, of beliefs and standards; it synthesizes all that commends itself to the American as the right, the good, and the true in actual life." The

American way of life freely uses the term, "god." Just witness any Presidential speech! But this god is a mere concept, never defined, and certainly not linked to Jesus. This amorphous theology was best expressed by President Eisenhower who noted that "our government makes no sense unless it is founded in a deeply felt religious faith—and I don't care what it is!"

The point Senator Hatfield makes in the introductory paragraphs to this chapter is that there are two faiths struggling for the allegiance of the American people. One of these is a little deity bound up with the American nation; the other is the biblical God revealed in Jesus Christ. Will Herberg says the American way of life is an idolatrous betrayal of the authentic Jewish and Christian faiths which find their beginning and end in God, who demands unconditional love and obedience and judges mankind's self-interest and self-aggrandizing pretensions.

Every Christian, wherever he or she lives, must be aware of the dangers of a culture religion. Christians in the United States have a particular need to sort out the genuine from the spurious if they are going to be faithful to the biblical revelation. Many so-called clergymen indiscriminately move from one faith to the other, seemingly unaware.

Former President Nixon was fond of describing the present anxieties and frustrations in the United States as a spiritual crisis. Indeed it is. As American power and culture collapse, we can expect the power structures to use religion in every way possible to justify their positions. Many persons will be beguiled by smooth words and a Madison Avenue religiosity. It will all fail unless it begins with "repentance," a word not found either in civil religion or the perversions of American Christianity.

8.

The future of America depends on...

LOOKING BEYOND OUR NATIONAL BORDERS

In the mass [people] acknowledge the legitimacy of the demands the national state makes upon them and accept the nation as the community which makes the nearest approach to embracing all aspects of their lives.—Rupert Emerson.

At the heart of the American Revolution was the decision of the early Americans to rule themselves. Along with a war for independence and a Declaration of Independence, the colonists began to think of themselves as a nation, a self-conscious peoplehood with a distinctive self-image and identity. No longer English, German, or French, no longer from Virginia, the Carolinas, or New England—but now Americans. Alexis de Tocqueville, a French commentator on American life, observed firsthand and marveled that "such a diverse group of 'spirits' could join together in certain common opinions."

From 1776 to the present this feeling of identification with the nation, the "I am an American" feeling, has risen and fallen, depending on the times. In

1776 Americans were one of the few peoples who were beginning to understand themselves primarily through the nation. In 1976 nearly all people around the world are nationalistic in the sense that the nation supplies them with identity and an outlook on the world. The "bicentennial question" is whether modern means of communication and transportation have made nationalism an outmoded concept, or whether modern weaponry and the experience of nationalistic wars require Americans and all peoples to consider new identities less bellicose and more interdependent.

If some such "new idea" is to develop, we must first understand nationalism itself. It is far easier to illustrate than to define. A clear, concise statement comes from an unknown Filipino politician who in pre-independence times announced "that he would prefer to go to hell with a government of his own than to heaven under alien guidance."

Self-determination is one of the key affirmations of the nationalist. In nearly as colorful a way, Jose Figueres added another dimension. To a U.S. House of Representatives Subcommittee on Inter-American Affairs, the former President of Costa Rica explained why then Vice-President Nixon was spat upon in Caracas, Venezuela, during his 1958 tour.

> But I must speak frankly, even rudely, because I believe that the situation requires it: people cannot spit at a foreign policy, which is what they wanted to do. And when they have run out of other ways of making themselves understood, their only remaining recourse is to spit. . . .

We are not asking for hand-outs, except in cases of emergency. We are not people who would spit for money. We have inherited all the defects of the Spanish character, but also some of its virtues. Our poverty does not abate our pride. We have our dignity.

What we want is to be paid a just price for the sweat of our people, the sap of our soil, when we supply some needed product to another country. This would be enough for us to live, and to raise our own capital, and to pursue our own development.

Nationalism includes a pride of culture and a quick resentment against insults from the outside. Numerous poems, hymns, and orations extol the nation. Nationalism filtrates and permeates nearly everything we do.

These illustrations suggest the varied content of nationalism. Definitions vary also. Carlton Hayes sees nationalism as "a fusion of patriotism with a consciousness of nationality." Hans Kohn, another noted historian of nationalism, calls it "first and foremost a state of mind, an act of consciousness ... the individual's identification of himself with the 'we-group' to which he gives supreme loyalty." Nationalism is based on the notion that humanity is naturally divided into nations and that the only legitimate type of government is national self-government.

Perhaps a better way to understand the term is to observe certain components of what makes up nationalism and nationality.

First is the concept of the nation as a community of people who feel they belong together. The nation is the larger community with which people most intensely and most unconditionally identify themselves.

A nation is usually made up of a people with a common language, culture, and history residing in a defined territory. These people have a special esteem for fellow nationals, stated so well by the Syrian nationalist Aflaq: "The nationalism for which we call is love before everything else. It is the very same feeling that binds the individual to his family, because the fatherland is only a large household and the nation a large family."

Such nations emphasize a uniformity of belief, the vague perception of a so-called national character, and a belief in a glowing future. Most nationalisms include a sense of mission, not only for their own society, but a manifest destiny for the entire world. In spite of such generalizations, it is important to recognize with Historian Boyd Shafer that "nationalism is what nationalists have made it," that it is very much a product of history —which means different qualities at various times and places.

"New nationalism" refers to the nationalisms of Asia, Africa, and Latin America: the nationalism of the Third World, primarily non-European in background. It could also include the black nationalism and Quebecer nationalism of North America.

The first element of newness is that this nationalism is basically anti-imperial, anti-colonial, and to a considerable degree anti-Western. President Nasser in 1956 pointed this up sharply. "Whenever we look behind," he said, "we do so to destroy the traces of the past, the traces of slavery, exploitation, and domination." These nationalisms are not necessarily spontaneous or self-generating movements. Rather, they focus on getting rid of the alien intruder and asserting a rediscovered or newly created identity.

This leads us to a second essential of the new nationalism: its revolutionary character. The older nationalism grew slowly along with the emergence of a new nation and frequently after a unified state was created. The new nationalism, an idea largely picked up under imperial tutelage, seeks to develop quickly all the trappings of modern nationhood. A whole new set of relationships needs to be established and older ones diminished or destroyed. The loyalties of a traditional society—religious, racial, familial, tribal, or caste—are reoriented to follow territorial boundaries. To be sure the desire to Africanize or to rediscover the antiquities and uniqueness of Ancient India or China may later materialize. But the first priority is to develop a sense of nationality and the structures of nationhood.

The impact of the West on the new nationalism has been enormous. This has included the idea of the nation and, more than that, the territorial entities themselves. Imperialists created Algeria from what had been the Barbary Coast. As recently as 1947, Chief Awolowo pleaded with the British to abandon their idea of a unitary state. For he said, "Nigeria is not a nation.

It is a mere political expression. There are no 'Nigerians' in the same sense that there are 'English,' 'Welsh,' or 'French.' "

Much of the new nationalisms' hostility to the West resulted from Europe's failure to live up to its own ideals. The notion of human equality was crushed in the obvious racism of the conqueror. The notion of political freedom was drowned in the repression of the freedom movements. The notions of humanity and fraternity were overwhelmed by the brutality of war.

Yen Fu, an educated Chinese, commented during World War I that "Western culture has been corrupted utterly. . . . It seems to me that in three centuries of progress, the peoples of the West have achieved four principles: to be selfish, to kill others, to have little integrity, and to feel little shame."

The new nationalism includes the pluralism or communal quality of their societies.

Particularly in Asia, religious and societal divisions are so strong that nations may divide on religious grounds (witness India and Pakistan).

The issue is simply, what should be our attitude toward nationalism? Is nationalism a hopeful development or the anti-Christ itself? Are there legitimate and illegitimate nationalisms? Is nationalism always a pagan cult or only sometimes? Can the universal church be authentically indigenous in a national culture and yet transcend it? Can Christians participate in authentic nation-building?

Whatever our answer, we must emphasize its reality. Hans Kohn calls our time "the age of nationalism." The new nationalism simply reflects that this is now a global force rather than merely a European phenomenon, and it is not merely political but extends to every institution of life. Arnold Toynbee observed not long ago that "today nationalism is about 90 percent of the religion of about 90 percent of mankind."

A key ingredient of nationalism is the myth of a noble past and a glorious future.

Our task is to understand why. E.U. Essien-Udom in his *Black Nationalism: A Search for an Identity in America* observes that the extravagant "eschatology" of the Black Muslims "expresses the nationalists's need to attach himself in a positive way to something worthy and esteemed, some center of power, some tradition and, generally, some central ideal capable of endowing his life with meaning and purpose."

Christians do well to recognize the Christian source of many nationalist ideas—certain beliefs about man, the chosen people, equality, justice, freedom, and the vision of a brighter future. In addition, the importance of history for the Christian is the root of much national historical consciousness. Many of these ideas, particularly in the Third World, were nurtured in Christian schools as any roll call of nationalist leaders can attest.

97

Nationalism is not merely an interpretation of reality, or an explanation of nationality, or even a lust for power. It represents a deep felt need on the part of modern man to belong, be affiliated. It offers hope of a meaningful life and relief from frustration and fear.

M.M. Thomas, an Indian Christian and an executive of the World Council of Churches, represents a widespread movement in Third World churches to advocate an active role for the churches in the building of the nation. While he insists there is no single interpretation of Asian nationalism, he senses three key ideas in his new nationalism. First, this nationalism frequently sees its mission as an instrument to spread Western democratic and humanistic ideas. Secondly, this nationalism serves as an instrument of theological development and economic productivity. Third, the new nationalism helps to develop a distinctive national selfhood with a national vocation in the world community. The new nationalism is thus a vehicle for creating modern culture, modern nations, modern men—an essential ingredient of modernization.

Is nationalism, as a search for meaning, a false religion? It would be easy to say yes. But before voicing such an opinion, we must not too quickly discount the idea of a nation. Even in the biblical record, nations appear to be part of the natural order as well as a punishment for human pride and self-sufficiency. The nations are judged, but they are also pictured as bringing their glory and honor into the city of God. For this reason we must recognize the legitimate aspirations of a people to control their own lives in freedom, with justice and equality. For this reason the church in Canada, Tanzania, and India, among other places, is properly concerned for national well-being. Indian Christians in 1960 said that "Christians, if loyal to their faith, should be fully involved in the nation's concern to be truly a nation, exercising its vocation as a nation among nations, and safeguarding its integrity against disruptive forces from within or without." M.M. Thomas sees national life as "an essential preparation of Asia for the gospel."

Nevertheless nationalism is always disturbing. Trevor-Roper, the British historian, is certainly correct in declaring that nationalism has been discredited and turned into a "dirty word" by fascism, Naziism, and imperialism. Any ideology which is intolerant in its exclusiveness, violent in its messianic zeal, divisive in its dogmatism, and, most of all, which subverts the "Holy nation"—the people of God—into disobedience to the great commandment, such a movement becomes a false religion. There will of necessity always be a continual tension, a persistent criticism, between the people of God and the peoples of nation states.

9.

The future of America depends on. . .

FOLLOWING GOD'S PLAN FOR THE WORLD

Christians must have a real grasp of the new situation of the universal Christian church in the present world; especially a grasp which springs from the intelligence of faith.—Henrik Kraemer.

There are a multitude of ways to perceive reality. Each nation or nationality understands current affairs from a British or Russian or Chinese or American point of view. The major world religions and ideologies propose explanations for understanding. Various social classes and racial and ethnic groups claim to unlock the secrets of human affairs. Every individual possesses a picture of human experience, a measure of hope for himself or herself and the family. Some of these images or pictures or road maps are simple and easy to comprehend; others are complex and difficult. Some people change their maps frequently, while others are prepared to die to defend their understanding of the times.

Perhaps the most widespread interpretation of the

times is that which each nation develops. Americans have a kind of creed which goes back to the Declaration of Independence and the Constitution. This statement holds that all men are created equal with certain unalienable rights—life, liberty, and the pursuit of happiness. Governments are instituted by men to preserve these rights; if government fails, a new government must be established. Americans believe in government under law, the balancing of power within governmental units, the free movement of a market economy, and guaranteeing religious freedom and minority rights. Americans hold that these qualities are good not only for themselves but for all people. They feel duty bound to defend and promote this vision.

Russians classically saw their own nation as "Holy Russia" with a providential role as a redeemer people. Since the revolution of 1917 and 1918, Russians have used ideas promoted by Karl Marx for understanding the world. This includes conflict between social classes —the haves and the have-nots—and the inevitable triumph of the oppressed masses. Nations with strong connections to the Christian church—Russia, England, and the United States—have often seen themselves as a chosen people and the rest of the world as an arena for redemptive national missions.

Within nations political parties and ideologies add other features to understanding the times. Liberals in the 1970s tend to want to use government agencies to expand the quality of life. Conservatives tend to be skeptical of large-scale social engineering, preferring to rely on voluntary agencies or private groups to resolve human dilemmas.

Wherever the nation or culture, whatever the religion, race, or political philosophy, all people have a road map in their minds which supplies them with certain values, a point of view, a means for understanding the times. It is difficult to determine which is more right or wrong, more accurate or more distorted. Sometimes these ideas are well developed; frequently they are not. Sometimes they are based on long study and observation. More often events take meaning from the orientation we bring to them.

For the Christian the events recorded by the historian or reported by the journalist are not "a tale told by an idiot, full of sound and fury, signifying nothing." Rather, they are ultimately related to what God has done, is doing, and will do in history.

This faith of the Christian rests on the knowledge that God has acted in events. The Bible records the story of how people reacted positively and negatively to these events. The Christian believes God still acts and desires response in an understanding of faith.

A Christian insight into current affairs results from a combination of careful analysis and the "intelligence of faith." This is a perspective, a way of looking at things, rather than a set of maxims which provide a ready evaluation of each action or event. John C. Bennett, former president of Union Theological Seminary, observed that in foreign affairs, "the Christian faith and ethics offer ultimate perspectives, broad criteria, motives, inspirations, sensitivities, warnings, moral limits rather than directives for policies and decisions."

The fundamental perspective is the affirmation that

everything which takes place needs to be understood in relation to the ultimate. This is God's world. He created, directs, and, finally, will end history. Man is a special creation made by God in His own image. The most important developments are those which involve the treatment of man.

Secondly, the Christian perspective recognizes the reality of evil. Man's response to God's actions have often been negative. The resulting sin has marred individuals and distorted society. All human institutions—political, economic, social, religious, educational—tend to be self-centered and lust for power. Power in itself is a tool but those who possess vast quantities can easily succumb to its lure.

There is, thirdly, a redemptive process in history. The definitive event, the very pivot of history, is Jesus Christ. The movement of redemption emanates from His life as the church witnesses to it. The love ethic personified by Christ is the norm by which all behavior can finally be judged.

History is also an arena of judgment. The biblical account of God's workings with man include both grace and judgment. Men individually, and the institutions God has created which had defied His will, have received and will continue to receive the wrath of Divine judgment.

These perspectives are validated in the biblical record. The Christian observer would be hard-pressed to label specific events as providence or judgment in the affairs of man. But the reality of evil and redemption offers us the basis for a faith which sees all these dimensions at work in the world of the bicentennial.

If the world is God's, the Christian observer begins by accepting history as a realm of utmost importance. The newspaper reports events which must be understood in the total plan of God.

If Christ overcame sin and death at the resurrection, then the forces of evil at work in the world are not decisive. Evil has already been conquered. History unfolds in the grace of God to provide continued opportunity for redemption. Reconciliation between men is a viable possibility.

The Christian who sees himself in the redemptive stream of history will tend to view the totality of human experience differently. He will strive to think outside the framework of the institutions whose power and future are limited. His values will be derived from the kingdom of God, not from his nation, political party, social system, or ideological explanation. The Christian stance will be one of detachment as well as involvement.

Love and redemption will be the Christian's chief concerns. The church will have a special role in the events of history as the focal point of God's redemptive activity. The global nature of Christ's lordship will provide a universal basis for evaluating events. The Christian will be as concerned about Peking as about Washington; Mao will be as much an object of his prayers as is Gerald Ford.

His judgment of events will include a passionate regard for human personality. Political platforms and economic systems will be evaluated by their impact on human welfare. These judgments will be made on ethical and moral principles rather than legal ones. For the law has an uncanny way of serving the status quo and the holders of power and privilege.

Finally, the Christian will expect to see history moving toward a cosmic consummation. The biblical story shows God leading man toward a goal. In the kingdoms of man and among the people of God there is an ever-present compulsion to preserve what is, rather than to build what ought to be. At moments like these, Herbert Butterfield observes, "Judgment falls heaviest on those who come to think themselves gods, who fly in the face of providence and history, who put their trust in man-made systems and worship the work of their own hands and who say that the strength of their own right arm gave them the victory."

The gospel is not only a set of perspectives. It is a way of life. It is a plan of action. Christian understanding of current affairs includes the obligation to voice a prophetic call to remind all men that Christ is Lord of Washington as well as of Geneva, of state as well as of church, of capitalist as well as communist, of white men as well as black, of Pierre Elliott Trudeau as well as Indira Gandhi.

It is no easy task to discern the meaning of events. Perhaps more than we like to admit, events take meaning from the orientation we bring to them. Bennett observes that even for persons with classified information such as the President, the secretary of state, and the secretary of defense, judgments are determined as much "by their broad pictures of the world" as by specialized knowledge.

The major events reported in the press—relations

between countries, the treatment of races, problems of poverty and affluence, ideological hostilities, and war—are moral issues. As such, the Christian must understand them through the eyes of faith.

10.

The future of America depends on. . .

MARCHING TO THE BEAT OF A
DIFFERENT DRUMMER

According to Christian social doctrine, there can be no genuine renewal of heart and mind without concern for social reform. Conversely, there can be no healthy and effective attempt to reform conditions without constant conversion of mind and attitudes. In this sense the true Christian is really the all-out revolutionary, the one who knows no rest or repose.—Bernard Häring

The collection of essays in this book is primarily concerned with understanding. It is important to recognize that understanding which does not lead to decision and action is self-centered and irrelevant. There are no simple panaceas for human dilemmas or obvious methods for resolving these problems. I do contend, however, that the demands of a common humanity require each individual to become, in some way, a part of the solution rather than a participant in the problem.

Political questions have always been an issue for the church. Jesus was a political figure. The early church grappled with political realities. Since the first century the church sometimes realized the significance of separation and exploitation. But too often the church has accommodated itself and oftimes gave a religious sanction to society as it was. The fact that there are political and social questions is a tribute to the impact of the church in inspiring among the masses of mankind an awareness that the way things are is not the way things have to be. Yet today as never before, the church confronts injustice, violence, poverty, and inequality not only as abstractions or societal evils, but also as realities that rend the church itself.

Christians who take both the world and their faith seriously sooner or later must reflect on the role of the church with regard to political and social issues. The International Missionary Council in 1947 put the issue succinctly: "Although the church has a life of its own, it touches at every point the life of the world and cannot disassociate itself from it, even if it would."

Though the church throughout its history has been close to and often deeply entrenched in political activities, few topics generate more tension in church life. Sometimes this is because political disputes are given such status that they divide congregations. At other times political and social questions are divisive because the membership is not sure that such issues should be debated by Christian disciples. Whatever the case, congregations rarely spend the time in study, prayer, and discussion necessary to develop a Christian stance on contemporary issues. The French Protestant theologian and scholar Jacques Ellul laments,

What troubles me is not that the opinions of Christians change, not that their opinions are shaped by the problems of the times, on the contrary that is good. What troubles me is that Christians conform to the trend of the moment without introducing into it anything specifically Christian. Their convictions are determined by their social milieu, not by faith in the revelation. They lack the uniqueness which ought to be the expression of that faith.

The Bible, the sourcebook for Christian insight, includes the political struggles of the kingdoms of Israel and the political dimesions of Jesus of Nazareth's birth and death. Indeed Jesus in His teaching and preaching used the political motif of the kingdom to summarize and focus His message. Jean-Marie Paupert, a French Roman Catholic author, observes that the idea of the kingdom of God carries an "evangelical political consciousness." Allusions to the kingdom of God in "its reality, its structures, even its very name, are expressed in terms modeled on a reality, a substance and a structure that is political and refer to them. Besides, the entry into this kingdom involves a kind of behaviour toward political realities, including economics, justice, and social relationships."

The Apostle Paul used the terms "new world" or "new order" to describe the status of persons reconciled to God and man (2 Cor. 5:17). The good news of the gospel is that man's brokenness, his separateness, has been overcome by Christ. His terms were like "Kingdom of God" itself, social and political ones. So also the bib-

lical term reconciliation, has to do with bringing opposi-
tions together. Reconciliation, Arnold Come says, "Is
God's act of working in and through all things together
in Jesus Christ so as to accomplish this one original
purpose in creation."

The New Adam has restored what collapsed with
the Old Adam. The apostle calls this a new creation, a
new world, a new order. Jesus announced the coming
of the kingdom. Whatever term we use, we are refer-
ring to the collective body of followers who have been
reconciled. Those who were "no people" now become
"God's people," the church.

The striking thing about the kingdom, the new
world, the church, is how it is imbedded in the
concrete realities of history. "As thou didst send me
into the world, so I have sent them into the world"
(John 17:18). Jesus lived among the oppressed people
of Palestine, preached a message that used the language of liberation, advocated a way of life destined to
challenge the accepted norms of society, and indeed died
because rulers saw in them a threat to the ecclesiastical
and political establishments of His day. This style, cul-
minating in the resurrection, was the style He expected
of His followers.

What does this mean for the church? It means first
of all following a different King. There is a difference.
The King isn't Herod or Caesar, Ford or Trudeau.
When such a choice is made, a clash is to be expected.
No one can avoid the cross fire. This is a kingdom
limited by no political boundaries, no economic qualifi-
cations, no ethnic affiliations. In this new world such
worldly distinctions no longer count.

Second, the new world is characterized not only by its Lord but also by its style of life. This new creation is made of individuals who have been made new, born again. Conversion means new relationships not only to God but to one's neighbor and to one's whole environment. This means not only living differently but thinking differently—as Paul says, "No longer from a human point of view." The new creation is not simply a collection of individuals, but a people who form a community so intense that where one suffers all suffer. For this community love is the motive force which creates harmony, justice, equality, and well-being in all its manifestations. Here is *Shalom*, come true out of a common obedience and surrender to God. Each person is subordinate to God and each other.

The details of this new world include a new politics, *nonresistance*, a new economics, *sharing*, and a new social order, *freedom to the oppressed*. Indeed the kingdom way of life affects every moral decision and every human and societal relationship. Andre Trocmé and John H. Yoder tell us that when Jesus in Luke 4 proclaimed "the acceptable year of the Lord," he was prescribing an ethic that continued the radical social reorganization that characterized the Old Testament year of Jubilee.

The beginning and end of the church's response to the social question rests on how faithful it has been as the new creation. The countenance of the church is indeed that of a sinner. The same countenance, paradoxically, is also the reality of a new creation. Of course there is need for continuous repentance and renewal. We must get beyond words to the painful process of self-criticism, self-denial, and genuine reform. Bernard Häring says it is only a purified church that will "be credible in a society yearning for liberation. The community of faith is more influential by means of presence and witness . . . than by means of social doctrine which does not reflect itself in the church's own life and structures." Helmut Gollwitzer adds, "If there is a failure in philanthropy even within your fellowship, then your philanthropy to people outside it will not be worth much either."

The heart and soul of the church's witness on social issues is the character of its own life. If racism exists within the church, any noble talk about the kingdom beyond caste is doomed to failure. If caste or class is present in the church, any talk about equality will be sneered at. If the church is part of the violent social order, no teaching on love and pacifity will be judged sincere.

The church confronts the social question as a new creation. The social question is overcome in the equality of life within the congregation and within the body of Christ around the world. The very existence of the church is her primary task. Hence the church must concentrate on not being seduced, on not capitulating to the evils of surrounding society. Another picture of the church's relation to political and social issues is found in the words of Jesus' Sermon on the Mount, "You are salt to the world. . . . You are light for all the world. . . . A lamp is lit. . . . where it gives light to everyone in the house." (Matt. 5:13-15, NEB).

The faithful church cannot avoid being a salt and light. As we have been reconciled, so we are agents of reconciliation. Only as we ourselves love and are peaceful and free can we preach love and peace and freedom. Then we can proceed to the task which Robert Cushman says "is not the harvesting of the reconciled out of the world but the extension of the reconciling task to the world."

What does this mean with regard to the social questions of our time—violence, militarism, racism, poverty, and cultural oppression? Rather than go into each specific, allow me to describe a way for the church to deal with a social issue which might be applied to any.

We begin by insisting that the foundation of any social witness is in being the church. A most important outcome of this integrity is the awareness by the people of God of what is right and wrong. Before any social question can be attacked, we need to have some clear notion of the ideal solution which for the Christian is the new creation. For this reason we need to work hard at studying what the Scriptures say, what Christ really meant. We need to listen to the Spirit's direction and consult each other since no one of us, nor any small group of us, has a complete picture of what God in Christ intends for the people.

Once we are aware of the truth and the good, it is necessary to critique the evil. One of the sad commentaries on our time is the dulling of our sensitivities. Many of us no longer can tell right from wrong. Describing evil in its bitter detail is almost as difficult as describing good. It takes prophetic courage and insight to do both. We of course recognize evil in our natural "enemies." The organized deception of modern propaganda mills, coupled with the deadening power of the mass media, means that far too many people do not comprehend the extent of racism, the facts of poverty, the grotesqueness of American weaponry, and the cultural and economic imperialism of Western Europe and America.

This critique and analysis is necessary not only for exposing evil but also to help the church be aware of the principalities and powers that control the "old world."

The church will confront specific social evils by conscientiously and systematically struggling against those that exist within its own ranks and, in so doing, deal with them beyond the boundaries of the faithful. This is close to our earlier comments on the church as a model society. But in the very process of keeping militarism and racism from affecting its life the church will have to recognize the structural dimensions of these evils. If the government imposes compulsory military service, the church will respond. If racial distinctions threaten to disrupt the church through legalized evil, the church will have to see that it stands in the world but not as part of the world.

The church will witness in private and public against the evils that surround it, forthrightly but always in a spirit consistent with the church's method and message. There are ethical norms for both ends and means. The church should know that it cannot overcome the devil by employing his tactics.

A major characteristic of such action will be concrete deeds which bear the burdens of the weak, share the sorrows of the oppressed, bless the poor, give to the beggars, love the enemy, lend expecting nothing in return, give homes to the homeless, food to the hungry, and clothing to the naked. Such social service is integral to being salt and light. But it is also important to recognize that charity must be complemented by the witness against those evils which make charity necessary. To be a Christ to one's neighbors means to speak and act with compassion to them personally but also to challenge the injustices that oppress them.

The striking fact of our time is the way nearly all problems—domestic and international—are tied up in some structural way. Speaking to racism, nationalism, militarism, and poverty means not only recognizing concrete facts and situations but also that these are bound up with each other. This not only requires an awareness of complexity but also a willingness to be salt and light to government officials and bureaucrats, to the corporation board and its executive officers, to the United Nations. One of the special roles for Christians who accept the viewpoint expressed in this book is a ministry of witness and dialogue to those Christians who accept alliances with worldly principalities and powers, reminding them of the whole gospel and the costs of discipleship.

Just as all problems seem to intersect with each other today, so also do all dimensions of the church's ministry. While at one time it may have been possible theologically and functionally to separate service (*Diakonia*), fellowship (*Koinonia*), and proclamation (*Kerygma*), now more than ever each is necessary to the other. If the church is on the defensive today, one reason is certainly that it has tried to accommodate itself to the world rather than being a new world willing to suffer for righteousness sake. Part of the accommodation process has been the separation of these ministries, emphasizing one over the other. As the popular slogan puts it, "You are either part of the problem or part of the solution."

The Christian task is to continue the kingdom announcement in all its fullness. When we pray, "Thy kingdom come, they will be done," we ought to reflect on the political significance of our request. Does it not mean we believe and witness to the conviction that people are more important than programs, that justice is to be valued before security, that equality for all people is to be cherished before any private fortune, that liberation is more important than the establishment of political power, that peace is to be sought before national prestige, that the church cannot be prescribed or limited by any political boundaries?

To quote Jacques Ellul once more, "Everything is political, but the genius and truth of the children of God is to have seen behind the political problem the real question: Who is the Lord?"

FOR FURTHER READING

Understanding the times takes study, reflection, and dialogue. Understanding is never complete but a moving on from point to point as new information and insight become available. Revision is the norm rather than the exception.

The reading suggestions listed here are primarily recent publications. Genuine understanding grows from a grasp of human experience in the past—history—and a recognition of the changing contemporary scene. The essays in this book are premised on the belief that biblical faith requires an understanding based not only on a descriptive analysis, but also on the Divine intention for people and the times. Real understanding becomes a prophetic inquiry into the human prospect and possibility.

The sources for prophetic inquiry begin with study of the Scriptures where the story of God and people during the ancient world is recorded. This must be supplemented by the teachings of the church, general historical works for background, and current journals and newspapers to document the continuing drama of people and the nations. Especially valuable are periodicals which try to understand contemporary realities from a Christian stance: *Christian Century, Christianity and Crisis, Christianity Today, Commonweal, National Catholic Reporter, Between the Lines, The Sojourners, Washington Newsletter of the Friends Committee on National Legislation,* and many denominational weeklies and monthlies. By no means are their interpretations the same!

What follows illustrates the broad range of literature available. Most of the volumes mentioned include suggestions for further reading. Many of the authors have more than one relevant book, but in most instances I have listed them only once.

Chapter 1

Peoples Bicentennial Commission, *Common Sense II,* New York, N.Y.: Bantam, 1975.
——, *Voices of the American Revolution,* New York, N.Y.: Bantam, 1975.

Chapter 2

James Mencarelli and Steve Severin, *Protest Three, Red, Black, Brown Experience in America,* Grand Rapids, Mich.: Eerdmans, 1975.
Gunner Myrdal, *An American Dilemma,* 2 Vols., New York, N.Y.: Pantheon, 1975.
Report of the National Advisory Commission on Civil Disorders, Introduction by Tom Wicker of the *New York Times,* New York, N.Y.: Dutton, 1968.

Chapter 4

Richard Barnet, *Roots of War,* New York, N.Y.: Penguin, 1973.

Francis Fitzgerald, *Fire in the Lake: The Vietnamese & Americans in Vietnam,* Boston, Mass.: Little, Brown, 1972.

John T. McAlister, Jr., and Paul Mus, *The Vietnamese and Their Revolution,* New York, N.Y.: Harper & Row, 1970.

Nguyen Knoc Vien, *Tradition and Revolution in Vietnam,* Washington: Indochina Resource Center, 1974.

Chapter 5

C.E. Black, *The Dynamics of Modernization: A Study in Comparative History,* New York, N.Y.: Harper & Row, 1968.

Jacques Ellul, *Violence: Reflections from a Christian Perspective,* New York, N.Y.: Seabury Press, 1969.

Irving Howe (ed.), *A Dissenter's Guide to Foreign Policy,* New York, N.Y.: Praeger, 1968.

Ronald Segal, *The Race War: The World-Wide Clash of White and Non-White,* New York, N.Y.: Viking Press, 1967.

Edmund Stillman & William Pfaff, *New Politics: America and the End of the Post-War World,* Mystic, Conn.: Verry, 1961.

Chapter 6

J. Anthony Lukas, *Nightmare: A Narrative History of Watergate*, New York, N.Y.: Viking Press, 1976.

Michael Novak, *Chosing Our King: Powerful Symbols in Presidential Politics*, New York, N.Y.: Macmillan, 1974.

Arthur Schlesinger, *The Imperial Presidency*, Boston, Mass.: Houghton Mifflin, 1973.

Theodore H. White, *Breach of Faith: The Fall of Richard Nixon*, New York, N.Y.: Atheneum, 1975.

Chapter 7

Robert Bellah, *The Broken Covenant: American Civil Religion in a Time of Trial*, New York, N.Y.: Seabury Press, 1974.

Robert Handy, *A Christian America: Protestant Hopes and Historical Realities*, New York, N.Y.: Oxford University Press, 1971.

Donald Kraybill, *Our Star-Spangled Faith*, Scottdale, Pa.: Herald Press, 1976.

Russell E. Richey and Donald G. Jones, *American Civil Religion*, New York, N.Y.: Harper & Row, 1974.

Chapter 8

Rupert Emerson, *From Nation to Empire*, Boston, Mass.: Beacon Press, 1962.

Charles W. Forman, *Christianity in the Non-Western World*, Santa Fe, N.M.: Gannon, 1971.

Carlton J.H. Hayes, *Essays on Nationalism*, New York, N.Y.: Russell, 1966.

Louis L. Snyder (ed.), *The Meaning of Nationalism*, Westport, Conn.: Greenwood Press, 1968.

Chapter 9

Richard Barnet, *Intervention and Revolution: America's Confrontation with Insurgent Movements Around the World*, New York, N.Y.: New American Library, 1972.

Daniel Bell, *The Coming of Post Industrial Society*, New York, N.Y.: Basic Books, 1973.

John C. Bennett, *Moral Tensions in International Affairs*, New York, N.Y.: Council on Religion & Innational Affairs, 1964.

Peter Berger, *Pyramids of Sacrifice: Political Ethics and Social Change*, New York, N.Y.: Basic Books, 1974.

Kenneth E. Boulding, *The Meaning of the 20th Century: The Great Transition*, New York, N.Y.: Harper & Row, 1964.

Lester R. Brown, *World Without Borders*, Westminster, Md.: Random House, 1972.

Herbert Butterfield, *Christianity and History*, New York, N.Y.: Scribner's, 1950.

Jacques Ellul, *The Presence of the Kingdom*, New York, N.Y.: Seabury Press, 1967.

Piero Gheddo, *Why Is the Third World Poor?*, Maryknoll, N.Y.: Orbis Books, 1973.

Denis Goulet, *A New Moral Order: Development Eth-*

ics and Liberation, Maryknoll, N.Y.: Orbis Books, 1974.

Robert Heilbroner, *An Inquiry into the Human Prospect*, New York, N.Y.: Norton, 1974.

Gary MacEoin, *Revolution Next Door: Latin America in the 1970's*, New York, N.Y.: Harper & Row, 1972.

Seymour Melman, *American Capitalism in Decline: The Cost of a Permanent War Economy*, New York, N.Y.: Simon & Shuster, 1974.

John Swomley, *American Empire: The Political Ethics of 20th Century Conquest*, New York, N.Y.: Macmillan, 1970.

Arend T. Van Leeuwen, *Christianity in World History*, New York, N.Y.: Scribner's, 1965.

John H. Yoder, *The Politics of Jesus*, Grand Rapids, Mich.: Eerdmans, 1972.

Chapter 10

Arnold B. Come, *Agents of Reconciliation*, Philadelphia, Pa.: Westminster Press, 1964.

Jacques Ellul, *The Politics of God and the Politics of Man*, Grand Rapids, Mich.: Eerdmans, 1972.

Bernard Häring, *A Theology of Protest*, New York, N.Y.: Farrar, Strauss and Giroux, 1970.

Jean-Marie Paupert, *The Politics of the Gospel*, New York, N.Y.: Holt, Rinehart and Winston, 1969.

INDEX

INDEX

126

THE AUTHOR

John A. Lapp is Dean of the College and Professor of History at Goshen College, Goshen, Indiana. He was formerly Secretary of the Peace Section of Mennonite Central Committee, Akron, Pennsylvania, and Associate Professor of History at Eastern Mennonite College, Harrisonburg, Virginia.

He attended Eastern Mennonite College, Case Western Reserve University, and earned a Ph.D. in British and European history at the University of Pennsylvania. In 1965, Lapp was a Fulbright Scholar in the Summer Institute in Indian Civilization in New Delhi. He has traveled in Latin America, the Middle East, Japan, Western Europe, and the USSR.

Since 1963 Lapp has written a monthly column on current affairs in *Christian Living* magazine. His major volume, *The Mennonite Church in India,* was published in 1972. He edited *Peacemakers in a Broken World* (1969) and has published numerous articles and book reviews.

Lapp is active in church, community, and educational affairs. Currently he is Chairman of the Mennonite Central Committee Peace Section (U.S.) and a member of the Commission on Institutions of Higher Education, North Central Association of Colleges and Universities. During the 1960s he was for a time President of the Rockingham Council on Human Relations, Harrisonburg, Virginia, and vice president of the Virginia Council on Human Relations.

He is married to the former Alice Weber of Lititz, Pennsylvania. They have three teenage children.